Keeping
CANARIES

Brian Keenan

THE CROWOOD PRESS

First published in 2012 by
The Crowood Press Ltd
Ramsbury, Marlborough
Wiltshire SN8 2HR

www.crowood.com

British Library Cataloguing-in-Publication Data
A catalogue record for this book is available from the British Library.

ISBN 978 1 84797 299 6

Dedication
The author and publisher do not accept any responsibility in any manner whatsoever for any error or omission, or any loss, damage, injury, adverse outcome, or liability of any kind incurred as a result of the use of any of the information contained in this book, or reliance upon it

Photographs: All the photographs in this book are by the author, except where specified otherwise
Diagrams by Caroline Pratt

Typeset by Jean Cussons Typesetting, Diss, Norfolk
Printed and bound in Singapore by Craft Print International

County Council

Libraries, books and more . . .

1 6 SEP 2013	1 7 MAY 2016	
1 4 MAR 2014		
- 9 MAR 2015		
2 5 JUL 2015		
1 6 SEP 2015		
- 7 OCT 2015		
14|.ə|.15		

Please return/renew this item by the last due date.
Library items may be renewed by phone on
030 33 33 1234 (24 hours) or via our website
www.cumbria.gov.uk/libraries

Cumbria Libraries
CLIC
Interactive Catalogue

Ask for a CLIC password

Contents

Preface

In compiling this book I have sought to provide an insight into the fascinating hobby of keeping canaries. My involvement with canaries spans over fifty years, since I first started keeping them as a young boy. Since that time I have made friends throughout the world, visited many foreign countries, and enjoyed the hospitality of friends whom I would never have met, had I not made my first tentative steps into bird-keeping all those years earlier.

Domesticated canaries are bred in a wide variety of colours, shapes and sizes, some for exhibition, some for their song, and others simply as pet or companion birds. Together, canaries are the most popularly kept domesticated caged bird, worldwide. They are fascinating creatures, and respond well to basic animal husbandry, being very adaptive and undemanding. As such, they are ideal for children, adults or the elderly, and will reward their owners many times over by their activities, companionship and song.

My own special interest is in exhibition canaries (specifically the breed known as the Yorkshire canary), which I have had the pleasure to keep since I was a small boy, and to judge in many different countries, meeting leading breeders and exhibitors on numerous occasions, with whom I have enjoyed discussing the intricacies of our mutual hobby.

Whether you intend learning more about canaries which you intend to keep as pets, or whether you plan to breed canaries or to venture into the competitive world of exhibition canaries, I commend this book to you, and trust you can benefit from some of the knowledge and experiences I have gained throughout my lifetime with birds.

If this book helps find one new devotee to canaries, then all the hard work and effort will have been worthwhile.

Brian Keenan, 2012

1 The History of the Canary

Canaries have been domesticated for several hundreds of years since the Spanish originally imported the wild canary from its Canary Isles home in the fifteenth century, attracted by its melodic song. Early attempts to control an expanding market failed when the Spanish mistakenly exported a shipment containing both male and female canaries to Italy, and from there canaries spread into countries such as Austria, Switzerland and Germany. Initially canaries were bred for their song, and even today, the Hartz German roller canary is highly regarded as the world's purest singing canary.

In the sixteenth century, canaries reached Great Britain. As the distribution of birds spread, groups of breeders set about producing specimens to their own liking, with shape, size and plumage given the most attention. They also devoted their attention to colour, and this was developed through selective breeding from the dull greenish-grey of the original wild canary to favour pale plumage, displaying much more yellow ground colour, until eventually canaries were being produced in the many different colours and 'breeds' that we know today.

Canaries in the twenty-first century are far removed from the wild birds captured six or seven centuries earlier. Now totally domesticated and 100 per cent dependent upon their owners for food, they would stand little chance of survival if they were returned to the wild.

Thus as we have seen, selective breeding was practised worldwide, and especially in Great Britain. Progressively, different geographic areas produced birds that broadly resembled

The common canary. People throughout the world have enjoyed keeping canaries since the sixteenth century. (Picture courtesy of George Zanias, Greece)

one another, but differed from those bred in other regions. This was understandable, given the difficulty in communication within countries, and especially across country boundaries. But within each locality breeders were keen to display their canaries, which led to the formation of local societies, so they had the opportunity to meet regularly and compare their stock. Different regions were fiercely protective of their birds, and in time regional societies were formed; guidelines were drawn up to rationalize the production and development of canaries so they conformed to certain breed standards, and this broadened the network of fanciers working along early breed model guidelines. This was the birth of the leading specialist societies as we know them today, and according to which our canaries have evolved to the high standards now seen throughout the world.

MAJOR ESTABLISHED CANARY CATEGORIES

Canaries are broadly divided into three categories: song canaries, coloured canaries, and type or posture canaries.

Song Canaries

Whilst all canaries possess a fine song, none can match the majesty of the German Hartz mountain roller for the clarity, variety and purity of its song. A popular canary related to the roller is the American singing canary, originally produced by crossing a border canary with a roller.

In Spain, the Timbrado canary is another highly prized singing canary; it is the newest of the 'song' breeds, originating around 1940–50. Said to be produced by crossing the wild canary with local Spanish song canaries, the Timbrado is gaining popularity as a singing companion bird.

The Waterslager canary from Belgium is another highly renowned song canary, with a song resembling the sound of bubbling water. With a soft to medium song, the Waterslager is reputed to have the widest range of all song canaries.

Coloured Canaries

While certain breeds of canary have been produced primarily for their song quality, others have been produced with the emphasis on colour.

Colour mutations exist in all branches of the canary fancy, based on the yellow and white ground colours. The coloured canary variety, on the other hand, has been produced by crossing a Black-hooded Red Siskin from Venezuela with a canary, with the intention of transporting the red genetic colouring of the siskin through any

Some canary breeders are interested purely in producing new colours through experimental breeding. The Red Mosaic canary is a prime example of the colour breeder's art. (Picture courtesy of George Ioannides, Cyprus)

fertile hybrids. These are termed F1 hybrids, and were mated back into the canary strain until a relatively pure canary emerged, with the ability to display a degree of red coloration in its plumage.

Over many generations, dedicated colour breeders have produced a whole new range of canary colours, which to a degree are not seen in any other pure-bred canary. Whilst the attempt to produce a pure-bred red canary has failed, the development of canthaxanthin (a colouring agent, commonly sold under the trade name Carophyll) has meant that the natural colour of the canary can be greatly enhanced, producing extremely attractive, richly coloured specimens.

Type or Posture Canaries

The third and by far the most popular and diverse group of canaries is referred to as the type or posture group. These canary varieties are distinctly different from each other, with the emphasis on a significant shape and size; these varieties differ from any other breed of canary.

This book concentrates on the leading type/ posture canaries.

A BRIEF HISTORY OF TYPE/ POSTURE CANARIES

On the continent, most development programmes favoured canaries with frilled plumage, such as the Parisian and North Dutch frilled canaries. Other breeding programmes worked towards the development of birds with an elongated neck and an erect stance: these became known as Belgian canaries. Developing the 'nerve', which was the term applied to the bird when encouraged to display itself to advantage in the show cage, was important for show purposes, because this enables the bird to draw out and extend its neck almost to the

Domesticated canaries are produced to exacting standards of excellence, and are far removed from their wild ancestors. This is a Gloster Corona canary, noted for its daisy petal head feathering, often humorously referred to as a 'Beatles haircut'. (Picture courtesy of George Ioannides, Cyprus)

point where it is making a number seven shape, an essential feature when the bird is in show position.

In Great Britain, type canary breeders developed their own speciality breeds; these were contained within the geographic limits of certain regions of the country. For example, the cotton mill workers of Greater Manchester developed a huge canary with an erect position. Ideally the bird was bred as a clear (*see* Glossary), being devoid of markings, although a grizzle marking on the head was acceptable. Because of the craze for size, many birds were paired buff to buff, and the bird became known as the 'giant' of the canary world, at more than 8in in length.

The popularity of the Manchester canary spread throughout Lancashire to such a degree that it became known as the Lancashire canary, and was available in both a non-crested and

The elegant Yorkshire Canary with its upright stance is known throughout the world as the 'Guardsman of the Fancy'. This picture shows a cinnamon yellow Yorkshire canary hen.

There are many varieties of frilled canaries worldwide. (Picture courtesy of Panos Paniagotides, Greece)

The Scots Fancy is an ancient breed developed in Scotland, and known as the 'bird of circle' as the distinctive forward head and neck position and hinged tail confirm. (Picture courtesy of Panos Paniagotides, Greece)

The giant Lancashire canary was developed by mill workers in Lancashire, England, and is often over 20cm in length, making it one of the largest canaries in the world. (Picture courtesy of Panos Paniagotides, Greece)

a crested form – that is, a bird with a shield-shaped crest known as a coppy. Plain-headed birds were known as 'crest bred' because they were produced by mating a coppy to a non-coppy bird, with an average yield of 50 per cent of both crested and non-crested birds.

In nearby Yorkshire, the success of the Lancashire canary had not gone unnoticed, and dedicated breeders in and around Bradford set about producing an altogether different, upright canary of their own. This was achieved primarily by mating Belgian canaries (because of their nerve and fine feathering) to Lancashire canaries. Occasional use of the Norwich canary was also made, to enhance colour. Ultimately birds were produced with much finer feathering than the giant Lancashires, and to guard against over-development and coarse feathering, a maximum recommended length was put into the Yorkshire canary show standard. Ultimately long, upright, elegant, slim canaries were produced, reputedly able to pass through a wedding ring: this was the Yorkshire canary, and because of its upright stance it gained the nickname 'guardsman of the fancy'.

In Norwich, Flemish refugee weavers brought with them their own favoured birds, larger than the average canary, and more portly. These evolved into the Norwich canary, known as the John Bull breed because of their squat stance and appearance.

Related to the Norwich, the crested canary is a somewhat coarser feathered, crested bird with a huge head in both crested and crest-bred forms. However, such has been the decline in the crested canary that it has been placed on the endangered species register, although it is being re-established in the UK with the help of a small band of dedicated breeders.

Another bird often accredited with Norwich ancestry is the English Cinnamon canary. This breed was derived in the late nineteenth century and closely resembled the Norwich, although it was perhaps a little larger. It has a distinctively rich cinnamon coloration, which

enthusiasts claim sets it apart from the Norwich and all other breeds of canary.

Not to be outdone, Scotsmen also developed their own breeds. The 'bird o'circle' is a rounded canary along the lines of a small Belgian canary, but with a tail that hoops under the perch, and a rounded back line; it is known as the 'Scots Fancy'. They also developed an altogether different bird, the active Border canary, produced in and around the border counties between England and Scotland. Over the years the Border canary has grown to such an extent that it now rivals the Norwich and Yorkshire canaries in terms of overall size – although many of its earlier exponents favoured a smaller bird, which led to the development of the Fife, originally a diminutive Border initially, but now a breed in its own right. The Fife has gone from strength to strength in popularity among canary breeders, largely due to its prolific nature, low cost and ease of management.

Still older breeds of canary exist, two of which are directly related. The Lizard canary has a distinctive plumage, with crescent-shaped rows of markings. Ideally the Lizard should be an entirely dark bird except for a clear cap, although there are broken-capped examples as well as non-capped birds; nevertheless the most distinctive feature of Lizard canaries remains the neat rows of markings, displayed best along the back, chest and sides of the bird.

Related to the Lizard, though not surviving much beyond the late nineteenth century, the London Fancy was a highly regarded, evenly marked canary with a dark tail. Various attempts to recreate it have met with failure, which is a great pity. A distinctive element of the London Fancy was that the chicks were all born as dark birds, but lost their dark body plumage as they completed their juvenile moult; the wings and tail retained the dark colour, however.

Much more successful has been the rise of newer breeds of canary, most notably the Gloster canary, a small cobby bird available in two versions, the plain-headed 'Consort' and the crested 'Corona'. In about 1925 Mrs Rogerson of Cheltenham in Gloucestershire took the leading role in the development of this bird, crossing crested Rollers with small Borders, with the intention of producing a miniature crested canary.

More recently Stafford canaries have emerged, the result of a coloured canary crossed with the Gloster, producing a red canary with a crested head. Another newcomer is the Irish Fancy, a snake-like, erect, mid-sized canary, which has gained many admirers because of its readiness to breed.

The latest new breed seeking accreditation is the Warwick canary, which although in its infancy, is already gaining admirers throughout the UK. We now have an established procedure by which the COM (*Confédération Ornithologique Mondiale* – World Ornithological Confederation.*)* accredits new breeds, and we wish the exponents of the Warwick canary every future success with their venture.

Overall there are canary breeds widely available to suit all tastes; these have earned a global following, and long may this be the case. Collectively, the humble canary remains the most popular of all caged birds worldwide.

Nesting canaries. Canaries are not difficult to breed, and most will make elaborate nests and raise young without problems. (Pictures courtesy of F. and M. Haerens, Belgium, and Panos Paniagotides, Greece)

2 The Responsibilities of Ownership

Keeping livestock demands a duty of care, which must be taken seriously. You will have no success in any sphere if birds are neglected, and they will obviously suffer if they are not cared for correctly, in a responsible manner. Caring for canaries is not a difficult task: animal husbandry of any kind is based on common sense, even in the twenty-first century when as many supplements are available as there are seed suppliers! All that is really needed is a little time and forethought, and regular routines for feeding, cleaning and management.

Remember, your canaries cannot ask for help – they can only depend upon you to cater for them, to the best of your abilities.

The essential areas of care may be grouped as follows:

- Accommodation
- Cleanliness and hygiene
- Feeding and nutrition
- General management

Seasonal changes must also be taken into account – for example, catering for your birds' needs when they are breeding is entirely different from when they are being exhibited – in order to provide a year-round care package for your birds, however many you keep.

ACCOMMODATION

Canaries are very accommodating and will thrive in a variety of locations. While

ABOVE: The interior of a well-planned birdroom. The room caters for the immediate needs of the birds and provides additional cage space for any new birds.

BELOW: Roof windows admit maximum light without wasting space.

the majority of exhibition birds are bred in birdrooms, just as many canaries are kept in aviaries, and still more as pet birds, generally in wire cages in the household living quarters. The focus of this book is on the care of exhibition canaries of all varieties, and their accommodation needs are discussed fully in Chapter 3.

Before embarking on any new-build project for a birdroom and/or aviary, consider how your hobby may expand over the next ten years or more; for instance if you plan to move house in that time, a semi-permanent or modular structure may best meet your needs. Overall, you owe it to your canaries to provide the most suitable accommodation you can in order for them to survive and thrive, and a little time spent planning before you embark on any long-term project will be time well spent.

CLEANLINESS AND HYGIENE

Animal husbandry of any type demands certain basic standards of hygiene, and this is as important for canaries as for any other animal. While clinical perfection is not required, reasonable standards must be maintained in order for the birds to remain in the peak of condition. The following practical aspects should be considered.

The Aviary

Gravel or flagstones are practical floor coverings, but will require cleansing and disinfecting at regular intervals. Soil can be incorporated into larger aviaries, and may even provide a home for some tender new plants and shoots; however, it will need turning regularly, so consider using it only in restricted areas.

If your aviary is open to the elements some form of drainage will be required, perhaps in

the form of a soakaway through gravel at one end.

Wooden surfaces should be tanalized or painted, and be sure always to use lead-free products. Rotten wood should be removed and replaced.

Aviary wires should be painted matt black, or should have a protective dark green plasticized coating; these will repel rust and last longer than standard galvanized products.

Birdrooms and Cages

A good quality lino floor covering is ideal, as it is easy to install, keep clean and disinfect. Ceramic floor tiles are hygienic, but are cold and hard on the feet, and can be slippery when wet.

For work surfaces, any standard kitchen

Nothing will reduce the condition of a canary quicker than a mite infestation. Thankfully, there are numerous readily available preparations which will have immediate effect on these unwanted pests.

This plastic cage front is a classic design with head holes for water and seed feeders and a centrally located door. It is readily available in a variety of sizes. Plastic requires little maintenance, will not rust, never requires painting and is easily cleaned.

worktop is ideal in the birdroom, and can be cleaned using standard household products.

The inside of cages should be painted with emulsion or gloss paint, or a water-repellent varnish, all of which can be washed down regularly.

In addition to household cleaners, specific birdroom products are available that guard against mites and provide relatively sterile conditions in which to house canaries.

Cage fronts can be made of wire, painted wire, stainless steel or plastic. My preference is for stainless steel or plastic because both avoid problems with rust, and are easy to keep clean and to disinfect.

Utensils

Utensils include all feed pots and feed stations, water pots, drinkers, fountains and baths, seed hoppers and finger drawers. A good basic rule is to wash and disinfect water pots daily, and it is good practice to have duplicate sets of water dishes so you can have one set in use while the other set is being washed and cleaned ready

for the next day. Water is most commonly the medium through which disease is transmitted, so cleanliness in this area is of the utmost importance.

In the same way it is good practice to have duplicate sets of soft food dishes and finger drawers, which will ensure that each new feed is provided in a clean dispenser.

D-cup water drinkers are often used on stock cages and the exhibition cages of a large variety of canaries, finches and other birds. Tubular drinkers are also a popular design as they prevent fouling.

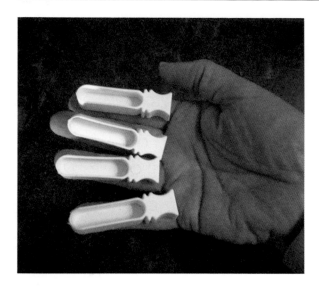

Traditionally used for feeding tit-bits, the finger drawer slides between the cage bars.

A good quality seed mixture should always be available to canaries, and is best housed in an external container, known as a seed hopper, to prevent fouling. The design shown has a removable Perspex side which is easily removed for cleaning.

Seed hoppers should be washed and cleaned weekly. It is amazing how much dust accumulates in a seed hopper, which if left undisturbed will provide a relatively safe haven for pests such as mite.

Perching

Perching of all description must always be kept clean, as it quickly becomes soiled, especially in flight cages and aviaries. Soiled perching can damage the relatively tender feet of canaries of all ages, and particularly those of younger birds. A bucket of household disinfectant is a simple way of cleaning perching in the weekly cage cleaning round.

Never allow perching in the cages to become damp or wet, as this will encourage the build-up of dirt and bacteria, affecting feet and potentially spreading disease. The 'spare set' rule applies as much to perching as to other items of birdroom equipment, and in the long run will improve birdroom hygiene, as well as simplifying the ongoing cleaning process.

Perching in aviaries may differ slightly, as many fanciers favour natural perches such as thin apple branches. Even so, new branches can generally be cut and replaced regularly during aviary cleaning operations.

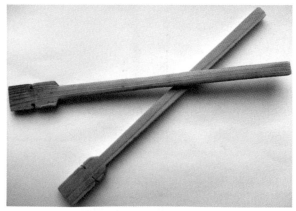

Softwood perches are ideal for canaries. The surface should never be too smooth, nor should it be round as this prevents a good grip. An oval box shape with the corners smoothed is ideal. The perches shown here twist onto the cage bars and do not require securing to the rear of the cage, which saves damaging paintwork, and reduces attacks by mites.

FEEDING AND NUTRITION

Feeding regimes for canaries should be structured according to the seasons of the year to ensure they are supplied with the nourishment that will meet their requirements in each season. The year is split into four quarters, as shown in the diagram, each with its own specific requirements. The most stressful times are the breeding and moulting seasons from April to September. The resting season, which is the show season, and the preparation season are from October to March.

First Quarter: Preparation Period

At the year start in January, a simple diet will keep canaries in good condition. This should consist of a standard mixed canary seed and daily fresh water. A proprietary soft food mixture should be given once a week during January, building up to two or three times a week in February and March in preparation for breeding. A teaspoonful of condition seed should be supplied once a week as a titbit.

At this time of year a source of calcium should be supplied in preparation for the following breeding season: cuttlefish can be

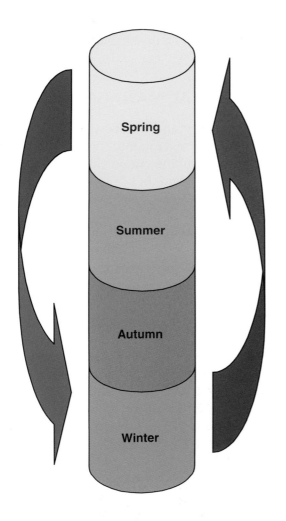

January – March
Lead up to the Breeding Season

April – June
Breeding Season

July – September
Moulting Season

October – December
Show Season

The canary calendar.

clipped to the cage or mixed into the soft food; alternatively many fanciers are now using one of several calcium additives. Grit can be scattered on the floor covering each time the cage is cleaned, which the birds will enjoy pecking through, or it can be supplied in a separate dish.

Vegetable matter and greenstuffs can be added to this feeding programme to ensure a healthy balanced diet: a little carrot, sprout, broccoli, lettuce, cress, or wild green foods if these can be collected safely. Some fanciers use supplements, but if you choose this option, use a company supplier that can provide sound advice to its customers, both at the point of sale and in the future, should problems arise.

Second Quarter: Breeding Period

From April to June is the canary breeding season: the diet as described above will meet the birds' basic requirements, though a more regular supply of soft food should be given to breeding hens, with the addition of soaked seeds. Whilst basic nutritional needs must always be catered for, the beginner should realize that there is no magic formula for success, and more experienced breeders may adjust their feeding regimes to suit their own circumstances and the needs of their birds, throughout the year.

Third Quarter: Moulting Period

In July canaries start moulting. This period has a special significance for those varieties of canary which are colour fed, as it is the only time that fanciers can effectively feed their birds foods that will confer added colour into the plumage.

This subject is dealt with fully in the section on moulting canaries. Soft food should be given throughout the moulting period as it contains

calcium, an important component in the production of new plumage.

The moulting period lasts until the end of September, and often into October and December for later born chicks.

Fourth Quarter: Resting Period (Show Season)

After the moult is over, all that is required is a basic diet of mixed canary seed and fresh water daily; this will bring the birds from breeding condition to show condition. Only a small amount of soft food need be given once a week, and little or no condition seed, until January, when the feeding cycle repeats.

GENERAL MANAGEMENT

Caring for canaries is best accomplished if you work to a routine. This routine will vary throughout the year to cater for their different seasonal needs, but can be tailored to match your own lifestyle and the time you have available each day.

It is good practice to make a chart for each season. On it, the daily tasks can be noted, which will ensure that all work is completed in a timely and efficient manner. The chart can be as simple or as complex as you require. An example chart is shown here. The tasks will change weekly, or by season, as required, and will act as an aide-mémoire until all the tasks necessary become second nature.

For those who take their duty of care seriously, these guidelines will ensure that all aspects of canary husbandry are accomplished efficiently throughout the year. No doubt experienced breeders will add their own items, or adapt the suggested tasks to meet their own criteria, but all will ensure that our charges remain well cared for and in the best of health.

A typical daily/weekly work chart

CANARY MANAGEMENT CHART		
JANUARY		
DAILY	**WEEKLY**	**JOBS THIS MONTH**
Seed	Soft food	Repair/paint cages
Water	Green food	Check breeding season supplies
	Fruit	
	Condition seed	
	Clean cages	
	Clean flights	
	Grit	
	Baths	

The above work chart can be as simple or complex as you require, but will help ensure every task is completed in a timely manner, until every aspect of canary management becomes routine.

3 Housing

Canaries are adaptable birds and will quickly settle into a variety of surroundings. Birdrooms vary from wooden structures, perhaps nothing more than a garden shed, to something more substantial built of brick, or perhaps a converted garage. It is also quite common to find that a spare bedroom has been designated as the birds' quarters.

BASIC CONSIDERATIONS FOR A BIRDROOM

A room free from draughts or damp is essential in order for canaries to thrive, and it should be as light and airy as possible. A clean air flow is essential for captive birds, but without being draughty, and to this end adequate air vents must be provided for the comfort of both the birds and the bird fancier.

Changes in temperature should be avoided, so it is best to dry line the room as a minimum, and provide some form of cavity insulation. The temperature should be maintained at around 40°F throughout the winter, rising during the summer when breeding is in progress: 60°F is a comfortable temperature to aim at to help maximize breeding results.

Selecting a Site

The birdroom should have good all-round access, adequate lighting and drainage, but be protected from the prevailing winds. Ideally it should enjoy the morning sunlight, but should be sited so that the mid-day sun does not shine directly into the cage. Do not worry unduly if these conditions cannot be fully satisfied: fanciers often have to compromise, and have always done so to good effect, probably ever since canary-keeping began.

Whilst some locations are more suitable than others, not everyone will have a choice. One of the most pleasing and successful birdrooms I have visited in the UK was purposely located under the shade of a giant tree. Not ideal you might think, yet that tree acted as a windbreak and provided much needed shade to the breeding room during the hot summer months. One complete side was made out of patio door-style double-glazing units, so light was never an issue, and a safety door prevented birds escaping when the birdroom door was left open.

Timber or Brick Construction

Both timber and brick have their advantages, brick-built structures offer low maintenance and a constant temperature, as against the portability and relatively lower cost of modular timber structures. Canaries will thrive in either type of structure, so the final decision has as much to do with personal preference as anything else.

It is imperative to check local planning and building regulations before undertaking expensive building works: a little foresight

With a little thought, birdrooms can be integrated into the overall garden design.

might save all sorts of problems later on. Regulations are different from county to county, so be guided by your local planning office.

The Roof

One of the most important decisions is the roof. A flat roof will often leak in later years, so if height is available, then an apex roof is preferable. The depth of the structure can also affect roof design, as a narrower birdroom can often take a sloping roof.

A permanent structure with a flat roof can accommodate raised roof lights, providing more daylight and saving on wall-mounted windows, so more cages can be fitted in the room. This can also be achieved with an apex roof, which furthermore has the advantage of providing storage facilities within the 'loft space'. It is amazing how much storage is required for items such as show cages, carrying cases and spare cage bedding, which can all be stored on site in the loft space. The loft need not run the length of the whole room, and with a little forethought, a pleasing design can generally be found to achieve the fancier's individual requirements.

The roof space should be insulated against undue heat loss.

Ventilation

Warm air rises and will be trapped in the roof area unless adequate ventilation is provided. The best design is an opening in the upper apex that runs the length of the roof, covered with perforated zinc on the inside and an inverted piece of guttering on the outside: this will provide protection against the weather and allow stale air to be released from the inside, to the benefit of both the birds and their keeper.

Air intakes should also be provided at a low level, fitted with control ventilators so as to avoid creating a 'wind tunnel' effect.

Modern fanciers can use a variety of products to improve air quality, including extractor fans and air ionizers, and these should be fitted in accordance with the manufacturer's instructions, and the size of the birdroom.

Insulation

Birdroom temperatures need to be controlled between about 40°F throughout the winter, rising to 60+°F in the summer months. Ideally there should be as little fluctuation as possible, and to achieve this, it is best to insulate the birdroom, either providing an air gap of about 2in, or filling this gap with an insulating material such

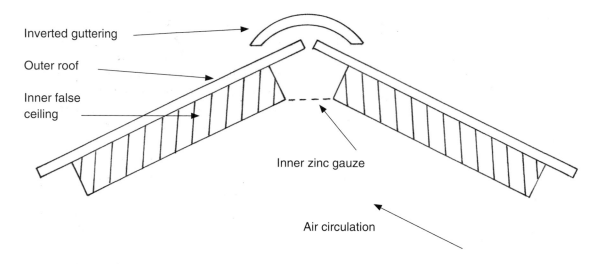

Inverted guttering

Outer roof

Inner false ceiling

Inner zinc gauze

Air circulation

Roof ventilation.

as expanded polystyrene, or some other proprietary insulation material, readily available at the local DIY store.

The initial expense of insulating the cavity gap will more than pay for itself over the lifetime of the birdroom on heating bills alone.

Heating

It is recommended to extend the central heating system from the house, or to provide low cost tubular heaters. In both cases, fitting a thermostat will ensure that the room remains at a constant temperature, to ensure the wellbeing of both the birds and the fancier. Too much heat may induce a moult, whilst too little results in water pots freezing during the winter months. When the birds are breeding, a temperature of 60°F will help to prevent egg binding, and is believed to reduce the incidence of dead chicks in the shell.

Lighting

Natural Lighting

As much natural daylight as possible should be allowed into the birdroom throughout the year, and the window design should maximize this facility. The benefits will be found during the summer months when the breeding season is under way, and also during the dark winter months, when minimal daylight is available. Double-glazed units are currently available at affordable prices, and these are preferable to ensure as little heat loss as possible. If an existing building is used, the installation of secondary glazing should be considered for the same practical reason.

Roof windows should be considered where practical, as these provide additional lighting, though of course they also increase heat loss. However, roof windows let in up to ten times as much volume of light as compared to a similar-sized side window, besides which more wall space will then be available, so more cages can be accommodated.

Heating is not essential, but both owners and canaries will benefit from a few degrees of warmth during the long winter months. Be sure to use a thermostat to control the maximum and minimum temperatures.

Artificial Lighting

Many fanciers now install electric lighting, which can be used during the long winter months to good effect, or when the birdroom is in the shade of other structures or trees. Tubular fluorescent lights are considered to be the most efficient form of artificial lighting, and full spectrum tubes that closely mimic natural daylight are preferable, rather than the false light provided by 'standard' tubes. However, bulbs are recommended as a back-up system because fluorescent lights cannot be phased on and off in the same way as an ordinary bulb.

When installing electric lights it is best to provide timer and dimmer systems, so that the length of 'daylight' can be automatically regulated; this allows the birds a natural roosting period before final 'lights out', and encourages them to feed before roosting, as they would do naturally if lights were not used.

Roof windows should be considered where practical.

Finally, a word of warning: electric lights may induce a 'soft moult' if used indiscriminately. Keep to a routine and all will be well, but using lights on an 'ad hoc' basis can be a recipe for disaster, ruining either a show season or breeding season, or both, if the fancier is not careful.

Doors

The birdroom door will be left open for most of the year, so an internal safety door is an absolute necessity, to keep cats and vermin out and your birds in. Ideally a safety porch is best, as this will reduce draughts and provide additional storage opportunities; however most rooms make do with a simple wire mesh closure. The outer door can be solid or contain glass,

which again will increase the availability of natural daylight if window space is at a premium.

Other Maintenance Items

The following basic items will also be needed in your birdroom:

- Airtight food storage containers
- Storage bins for items of perching, feeding utensils, birdbaths and so on
- Brush and shovel
- Mop and bucket
- Waste water bucket
- Rubbish bin
- Workbench or work surface

CAGES AND CAGE UTENSILS

Cage Design

Canary stock cages are generally of a standard box design 14in (35cm), 16in (40cm) or 18in (45cm) wide and 12in (30cm) high, and between 10 and 12in (25 and 30cm) deep. The cage front is usually fitted into a top and bottom rail. Most breeders favour a double or treble breeding cage, which can be divided by slides to provide single cages, or a double-/treble-length breeding or flight cage. Canaries are accommodated in small or large cages according to their size.

Cage Furniture

Cages are generally equipped with oval perches made from softwood, which will not injure the birds' feet, and standard seed hoppers and water pots clipped to the outside of the bottom rail of the cage.

BIRDROOM DESIGN CONSIDERATIONS

- Provide as much ventilation as possible, but keep free from draughts
- Provide as much natural light as possible
- Protect the structure from prevailing winds
- Ensure a constant temperature by insulating the structure where possible
- Protect from sudden lights from cars, houses and street lamps
- Plan for power supplies for lighting and heating
- Plan if possible for water supplies with draining, where practical
- Ensure access all around the structure, to allow for future maintenance
- Keep away from draughts
- Raise wooden structures off the ground
- Ensure the structure is watertight, and free from damp

This birdroom utilizes blocks of cages, equipped with continental fronts that incorporate an additional cage door. (Picture courtesy of F. and M. Haerens, Belgium)

Cages are built directly into the birdroom walls in this room and, by withdrawing the separating slides, can be used as extensive flight cages.

Seed and water containers are generally hooked onto the outside of the cage rail, for ease of access and to help prevent fouling.

Cage Floor Covering

Most fanciers use sawdust or wood shavings as an absorbent floor covering, changing this at regular weekly intervals. Newspaper is a useful alternative covering, for example if the canary keeper suffers from a dust allergy.

Baths

Baths that hook on to the cage door are essential, and will be used regularly by the canaries to help keep their feathers in good condition and free from unwanted pests. The canary's feathering acts as an insulator, and birds in good feather condition will withstand the rigours of a long wet winter

There is no better conditioner than a bath every morning. Each of these cages has its own bird bath attached.

This item, originally designed to clip cuttlefish bone to the cage wires, is useful for nesting material, green food and numerous other purposes, such as holding information notes or privacy boards, when the hens are incubating eggs or nesting.

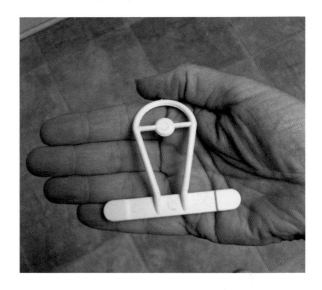

far more readily than those with dirty, soiled plumage.

Feeding Utensils

Essential feeding items include egg-food drawers, which hook under the cage door and are used to supply soft food or soaked seeds as required, and finger drawers which slide between the cage wires and are used for feeding condition seed or other treats. Cuttle clips are used to hold cuttlefish bone, or as a fastener for green food, holding it against the cage front for canaries to peck at. These clips can also be used to offer nesting material during the spring and summer months.

Breeding Season Equipment

Standard canary nestpans should be

Rings are available in a variety of colours, and are easily applied or removed using the aluminium tool supplied. Split rings are primarily used for identification purposes.

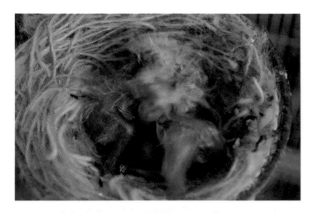

A nest of young canaries which have been rung using closed rings while still in the nest. (Picture courtesy of George Ioannides, Cyprus)

provided throughout the breeding season, at least two per hen. Suitable nestpan liners are also essential at this time. A good supply of plastic canary eggs is required for when the hens start to lay eggs, and of course the rings of your choice, either closed or split rings, as necessary. Ringing canaries is for identification purposes, and it is generally the breeder's personal choice whether to ring or not. Open rings can be applied at any age whilst closed rings can only be applied when the birds are a few days old and still in the nest.

Training Cages

Even if it is not your intention to exhibit your canaries, show cages are essential, both for moving the birds around when cage cleaning work is in progress, or to train them to become more friendly, or steadier for exhibition purposes. Most fanciers keep a few old cages for training, with the better cages reserved for the show bench.

Young canaries enjoy regular outings in training cages, which are shown here affixed to the stock cages in which the birds live. (Picture courtesy of Tony Ruiz, USA)

4 Nutrition

Feeding and management are the daily essentials of good canary husbandry, and fanciers should establish a fixed routine to ensure their birds receive proper care and attention throughout the year. This routine need not be too elaborate, but it does need to reflect the seasons of the year, which coincide with the needs of birds throughout their life cycle, as discussed in Chapter 2.

Each season requires a slightly different feeding approach appropriate to the time of year in order to maintain the birds' health. This allows your birds to accustom their metabolism to the appropriate season, ensuring they are brimming with health at the appropriate time in order to breed, moult or rest. Adopting this type of approach will ensure not only the fitness and wellbeing of your stock, but will also lay the foundations for a successful breeding season, which is the climax of the canary fancier's year.

THE MODERN FEEDING APPROACH

Canary feeding has changed greatly during the latter part of the twentieth and early part of the twenty-first century. Our forefathers had only their own instincts to guide them, and only a limited range of commercially available seeds and egg foods. Earlier fanciers consequently produced their own home-made soft foods, and supplemented their birds' daily feeding with wild seeds, grasses, fruits and berries. Considering the average disposable income in the late nineteenth and early twentieth centuries, and the hardships endured throughout the war years, it was this inventiveness that helped to ensure the overall survival of many of the established canary breeds, which are the forebears of several of our current leading studs.

Today the world has changed dramatically, and for many modern birdkeepers the proven management approach of our ancestors is no longer viable. One reason is that the level of pollutants extensively poisoning our national countryside – the effects of transport and agricultural pesticides, to name but two – has increased to such an extent that gathering wild foods can potentially put the birds' health at risk. In addition, the pace of modern living means that many people simply do not have the time to spend on regular foraging expeditions.

In compensation for this, the bird food industry has grown considerably, and today the huge choice of feeds and commercial supplements is positively bewildering. We are also much better informed concerning bird nutrition, and a variety of companies both at home and abroad can now supply a far wider range of seeds, seed mixtures, soft foods and supplementary products than was ever available in the past. The task facing the modern fancier is to provide a balanced and varied diet that meets the birds' nutritional needs throughout the year. Each group of foodstuffs is outlined separately in this chapter, together with advice as to its usage throughout the year.

Basic Food: Seeds

Canaries are seed-eating birds, which means they can be successfully maintained during their resting periods on a diet consisting mainly of dry seeds, and of course a regular supply of fresh water. Feeding dry seed is particularly convenient for fanciers with little time to spare during the week, because any extras can be given to their birds during the evenings or at weekends, as appropriate. Equally, if the fancier has to be absent for a few days, neighbours, family or friends will have absolutely no difficulties in looking after the birds until he returns.

The following paragraphs describe the most commonly available seeds and their uses.

Canary seed is blended with small proportions of other seeds to provide a basic all year round seed mixture. This mix contains black rape seed, linseed hemp and biscuit in addition to plain canary.

Canary Seed (Phalaris canariensis)

The staple canary diet uses canary seed as a

Canary seed forms the staple diet for canaries. Always look for a healthy sheen on seeds, which should be plump to the touch. Avoid any dusty, stale or mouldy seeds of any kind that could be harmful to your birds.

base, and it often forms between 60 to 90 per cent of the total mixture. Canary seed (or canary grass) is native to the Mediterranean and the Middle East, though recently the major producer of canary seed has been Canada. A larger seed was produced in Morocco, and this is much sought after by canary breeders.

Canary seed should be firm, even solid when felt in the hand, and sweet smelling, with no sign of mustiness. Clean seed shines as if polished, and there should be no dust on it.

Today, many seed suppliers kiln dry their seeds, which can lead to a reduction in germination. As a consequence, some canary breeders now purchase seeds from different sources in order to balance the overall seed quality and guard against feeding nutritionally poor seed to their birds. Since plain canary seed forms the major part of the canary diet, comprising at least two-thirds of any seed

The following seeds are often added into rearing foods. From top, niger, sunflower hearts, teazle and hemp.

mixture, it can be appreciated why fanciers will go to such lengths.

Rape Seed (Brassica campestris)

Brassica campestris is a species of wild cabbage, but the commercial rape seeds that we buy today are varieties of what is commonly called oilseed rape. This crop can be seen extensively throughout the British countryside in May each year, shining bright yellow in the fields.

The best varieties of rape seed are German rape and Rubsen rape. This seed is a reddish purple-brown in colour, with a yellowish kernel. It should have a pleasant, nutty taste, and should not taste bitter or hot. Rubsen rape is a larger rape seed and is very mild in taste.

Some canary breeders serve cooked rape to their hens as a rearing food: the seed is boiled for about ten minutes, and then rinsed in cold water.

Niger Seed (Guizotia abyssinica)

Niger seed is also known as niga, inga or nigra – the word simply means 'black'. Niger is the seed of a plant closely related to the sunflower. It is largely grown in northern India for its oil content – it contains almost 40 per cent oil by weight – and is manufactured for soap, or for oil for use in lamps. The seed is about 4mm in length, and like all seeds should only be bought if it is shiny black and smells clean and wholesome. Only the current season's crop should be bought, and stored seed should always be used within a season and disposed of at the end of the year.

Nineteenth-century canary expert C. A. House wrote:

[Niger seed] is a grand seed and I have used immense quantities of it during the cold winter and spring months. Some fanciers only use it during the breeding season; I use it all year round. Birds will leave any other seed for Niger, they will even abandon Hemp. Although it is rich in oil I have never known any ill effects from its use, and for keeping birds in good health and full song there is no seed to equal it.

Although not strictly a supplement, conditioning seed can be used in small quantities as a tonic throughout the winter. Generally speaking, conditioning seeds are too rich for everyday use.

hemp – although take care not to grind up the shells of the seed with the kernels, since this is said to contain small amounts of an irritant poison.

Hemp can be soaked and sprouted and given to feeding hens in moderate amounts. Soak for twenty-four hours, rinsing regularly, and feed when the white shoot begins to crack the seed coat.

The Birdman of Alcatraz, Robert Stroud, believed that 'in small quantities, hemp is one of the most valuable foods for canaries since it is rich in oils and in vitamin E.' Robert Stroud (1890–1963) served a total of fifty-four years incarcerated in various US penal institutions, having failed to obtain his release from an originally harsh twelve-year sentence. During this time he wrote two works on the diseases of birds. His book *Stroud's Digest on the Diseases of Birds* is still regarded as a classic ornithological work. Stroud used hemp to bring birds into breeding condition.

Hemp Seed (Cannabis sativa)

Hemp was grown widely in the UK and America for centuries as a source of weavable fibre, used for making ropes and coarse cloth. One variety of hemp plant is the source of marijuana and the condensed resin – cannabis – hashish, an illegal narcotic drug. However, other varieties of the same plant do not secrete the psycho-active drug, and these are the source of commercial hemp seed.

The best hemp seed is greyish brown in colour, often with a slightly green tinge. The kernel is white and has a sweet, nutty taste. Hemp is a very strong seed (try cracking it with your teeth) and it is amazing that adult canaries are able to crack the shell unaided, rolling it in their beaks before cracking it.

Hemp can be partially crushed with a rolling pin, and young birds will benefit from crushed

Another seed often added to soft food, maw seed is thought to have relaxing properties for canaries. It is easily digested by young birds.

Maw Seed (Papaver somniferum)

Maw is the seed of the opium poppy. The word 'maw' is Old English for 'mouth'; it is also related to 'crop' or 'craw'. There is no such plant as 'maw' – the term simply points to the use of the seed as bird food. The opium poppy is the source of opium, morphine and heroin, but the seeds contain such a minute amount (if any) of the drug as to be harmless.

Maw seed is pale blue and should smell fresh and sweet. It is very rich in oil, so buy only new-crop seed and use it all within a season, and dispose of any surplus at the end of the year.

Richard Morse (author of *Wild Plants and Seeds for Birds – An Illustrated Dictionary of the Best Foods for use in the Aviary*) wrote:

> Maw is one of the most valuable seeds for the bird keeper. It is practically the first seed the young bird eats on weaning, and in the final stages of senility, the old bird seems to relish a little maw seed more than anything else.

C. A. House, who was a highly-regarded authority on canaries, and editor of *Cage Birds* weekly magazine at the turn of the twentieth century, wrote:

> It is very nourishing and comforting, being rich in oil. Its medicinal properties are very great and it will often cure diarrhoea without the aid of any other drug.

Linseed (Linum usitatissimum)

Linseed or common flax has been grown since biblical times as a source of fibre for the production of fine linen. The mature plant is traditionally steeped in water until it decays and the strong fibres can be separated from the stem; they are then bleached, and spun and woven into linen.

Linseed is an oily seed, used when canaries are moulting to add a sheen to the new plumage.

The seed is fed to racehorses to improve the appearance of their coat, producing a beautiful gloss. It is also said that to improve a horse's stamina.

Canaries will often ration their intake of linseed, probably because it is very rich and oily. It is also rich in protein: according to Richard Morse it contains over 100 grains of protein to the ounce, as compared to a hen's egg which contains only 60 grains of protein to the ounce. It is included in general seed mixes as a minor component. C. A. House wrote:

> It is a grand demulcent, softening and mollIfying any inward irritation of the intestines; further, it is a splendid seed for keeping birds in the peak of condition, producing as it does the wonderful lustre and beautiful brightness of plumage that is so much sought on the show bench.

Enhanced Seeds or Pellets

Becoming increasingly popular, new scientifically blended pellets are being offered to our birds, in addition to a plain seed diet. These pellets resemble small round seeds, such as millets, but are available in a variety of different colours, which denotes their properties. This enables the fancier to provide an enhanced yet balanced diet, which is readily taken by the majority of canaries, after an initial settling-in period.

This is an advance not only in feeding seed-eating birds, but also in supplementation, and will undoubtedly increase progressively in future years.

Soaked and Sprouted Seeds

Soaked or sprouted seeds can take the place of wild green foods. When I first started breeding canaries I lived in a rural area, and gathering wild seeds and grasses from the fields and roadsides was not a problem. However,

increasing urbanization and the widespread use of pesticides made me rethink my feeding methods, and I came to the conclusion that wild seeds and green foods were no longer a viable option. Today I rarely feed wild green foods at all, other than in the form of sprouted seeds.

There are many seeds that are ideal for sprouting. Rape seed forms the basis of most commercial sprouting mixtures, but other excellent seeds are mung beans, hemp, sunflower hearts, oats and teazle.

I use plastic seed germination trays with a solid base in which to soak and sprout the seeds. These trays fit comfortably on to my birdroom worktop, close to the window. I cover the seed with cold water, having added a few drops of aviclens or household bleach to the water to help rid the seed of unwanted bacteria or yeasts. This mixture is left soaking overnight until the next morning, when the contents are poured into a large sieve and thoroughly rinsed under the running tap for a few minutes.

Bleach or avian disinfectants serve a very important purpose. During soaking the seeds undergo a chemical change, in which their contents are changed into simple sugars. This means they are prone to infection by fungus, yeasts or other such-like killers, so it is worth considering the addition of cleansers – never forgetting to rinse thoroughly after the initial soaking, and always immediately prior to feeding.

After the first day's soaking the sieved seed is rinsed thoroughly, then suspended in a sieve over a drip tray, and a fresh batch of soaked seed is prepared in the original seed tray. Throughout the second day I run the sieve under the tap several more times, and under normal circumstances by the end of the second day the seed is beginning to sprout – known as 'chitting' amongst birdmen. I find that by the end of the second day 'in the sieve' small seed sprouts can easily be seen, and sometimes during hot weather this occurs more quickly.

After a final rinse the seed is ready to feed to canaries, and is always eaten with relish. The three-day preparation cycle soon becomes routine, and the amounts being prepared can be increased, depending on your needs throughout the breeding season.

It is a matter of personal choice whether the sprouted seed is fed separately, or used to dampen down the soft food you will also be feeding to your stock during the breeding time. My preference is to feed the seed separately, as the birds will scatter the soft food as they search for their favourite sprouted seeds, and so the second dish is far more 'cost effective' in the long run – even though it doubles the washing up!

The golden rule is to feed sprouted seeds little and often, adjusting the timing of feeds to suit your own convenience as much as the needs of the birds, which will adapt to suit you. If they can rely on a regular feeding regime they will be happy.

Soft Foods

Whilst seeds form the staple diet of canaries, this is enhanced throughout the year by the provision of soft food. Soft food is offered as a general conditioner during the resting period following the completion of the moult, but only in small quantities, once or perhaps twice per week. At the turn of the year when the stock is being conditioned for breeding, soft food is offered increasingly – twice, three or even four times a week – until the birds are introduced into their respective breeding cages, when daily supplies of soft food can be provided.

During the rearing period the old maxim of little and often is the general rule, with freshly made soft food offered to the feeding parents, three or four times per day.

There are many commercial brands of soft food offered on the market, which take two basic forms: a dry soft food,

Good quality soft food is essential when breeding canaries. Commercial mixtures are readily available, or home-made recipes such as this one are often used by experienced breeders.

which is moistened before use, and a ready mixed soft food, which does not require moistening.

In addition, many fanciers have their own private recipes, often based around a rusk or bread/biscuit base, to which eggs and fruit/vegetables are added, plus a small amount of niger and maw seed. My own current preferred recipe for home-made soft food is as follows:

- 1 teacup dry sausage rusk
- 1 eggcup porridge oats
- 1 teaspoonful honey
- 1 teacup water to blend together
- 3 hard-boiled eggs, grated into the mix
- 1 medium carrot, diced
- ½ sweet apple, diced
- ½ cup garden peas (frozen, defrosted in hot water prior to use)
- ½cup sweetcorn
- Maw seed and niger seed

The above will make one large bowl of soft food sufficient for forty canaries, and if stored in the fridge will last for approximately two days during the normal breeding season. The mix is eaten with relish. I usually start this during the winter months, then feed more regularly from January, to help the birds attain breeding condition.

Minerals and Grits

No diet is complete without minerals and grits, used to provide calcium and aid digestion. Sharp sand, mineralized tonic grit, oystershell grit, charcoal, seaweed and crushed dried eggshells are all perfectly acceptable sources of grit which should be provided regularly.

Cuttlefish bone is an accepted form of calcium, either fitted into the cage or scraped and blended with the soft food.

Vegetables and Fruits

Canaries will benefit from a varied diet, and will take most fruits and vegetables quite readily. These foods act partially as a replacement for the natural wild seeds and grasses which modern-day bird keepers are generally unable to use for a variety of reasons, as outlined earlier. The more common fruits used are apples and oranges, whilst garden peas, Brussels sprouts, cabbage, carrot, broccoli and cauliflower are all eaten with relish by most canaries. In season, pumpkin is accepted in small amounts, being both sweet and moist.

Commercial or easily grown green foods that will be taken include watercress, mustard and cress, lettuce, spinach and rocket salad.

Wild Seeds

Those fanciers choosing to collect and feed wild seeds and grasses generally seek out the following:

- dandelion
- chickweed

Grit forms an important part of the digestive process, and should be available to canaries at all times.

- plantain
- fat hen
- shepherd's purse
- rye grass

Each wild food is beneficial, particularly as a conditioner, with most fanciers acclaiming the humble dandelion (buds, flowers, leaves, root, milk seedhead and dried seedheads) as being of particular use throughout the year.

Care should be taken when offering chickweed during the breeding season, which is a particular favourite of canaries feeding young. Always ensure that you have an adequate source throughout the breeding season, in order that the birds continue rearing on this preferred wild food source. Should the source dry up, it can be extremely difficult to coax canaries on to another food supply.

Supplements

Modern fanciers have a distinct advantage over their earlier counterparts, in that there are innumerable supplements and additives available to them, many of which are commercially available worldwide.

Whilst a varied diet and access to the necessary minerals will obviate the need for many supplements, the fact remains that birds kept indoors will automatically miss essential items from certain areas of their diet, which will affect their ultimate wellbeing – for example sunshine and vitamins.

The best advice regarding supplements is to discuss your birds' performance, and hence identify their needs, with a reputable supplier. Several suppliers will provide detailed feeding regimes using individual supplements and a programme designed to meet the birds' needs at different times of the year. Talk to several suppliers to obtain advice, and check this advice with known successful fanciers using the various products identified. In this way you will be able to make a better informed decision, and the results you achieve will be measurable in terms of your birds' improved performance in the breeding room.

Cuttlefish bone is traditionally used as a source of calcium. Canaries will often rub their beaks onto cuttlefish to help keep them from becoming overgrown. In addition, liquid calcium is a favourite supplement used by many birdkeepers, fed through the drinking water, mixed in soft food or diluted onto fruits.

SEASONAL FEEDING AND MANAGEMENT PROGRAMME

The foregoing feeding information satisfies the basic requirements of feeding and managing canaries successfully throughout the year. A successful seasonal programme is described below.

Spring (January to March)

Spring is the lead-up period to the breeding season. From a management point of view the shows are over, all spare stock has been disposed of, and the remaining stock that you intend to breed from should be conditioned in such a way that they attain peak form at the commencement of the breeding season.

There are several tasks that warrant attention throughout this important period January to March. Do not leave everything to the last minute, and remember that your birds will only perform successfully if they are properly prepared, in a timely manner.

Feeding

There are two distinctly different feeding approaches which depend on the time available to the fancier, and how easily green foods can be obtained. The different approaches relate to diets that are supplemented by natural or alternative products in order to maintain peak health and condition. Most modern fanciers supplement their birds' diets to a greater or lesser extent, as outlined below.

When feeding in the spring the overall aim is gradually to improve the birds' condition to ensure they arrive in full breeding condition during March and early April. Increase your vigilance when out and about during this period to uncover early dandelion, which can be gathered, washed and fed – roots, flowers and all – whenever available. Always feed in small quantities so that no stale food is left in the cages, in between the weekly clean.

Seeds

A good quality mixed canary seed, available from any of the leading commercial suppliers, should be provided daily. Try to ensure that the product used is clean and free from excessive dust. It is also advisable to purchase from an organization with a regular, quick turnover, so you are not buying old stock. The main seeds in a mix will be plain canary and rape seed, with small amounts of hemp, linseed and niger, all generally added to the mixture by the manufacturer.

Canary seed contains over 50 per cent starch, whilst rape seed has over 40 per cent oil and fat content; this therefore provides the basis of a balanced diet, used successfully by canary breeders throughout the UK for over 100 years. Most seed merchants add other seeds into their mixes, and the fancier may choose to increase slightly the amount of plain canary seed.

A teaspoon of condition seed can be fed twice a week: this helps to increase the birds' protein, fat and oil intake as the preparations for the breeding season start to gain momentum in January. Increase the condition seed slightly to, say, three times a week from February and throughout March.

Minerals

A regular supply of a good grit mixture should always be provided; it should contain mineralized grit, oyster shell grit and a little charcoal, and can be sprinkled on the cage floor each time it is cleaned, where the birds will immediately peck it over.

Cuttlefish as a form of calcium should also be provided, either separately, or powdered and mixed into the soft food, each time this is fed.

Soft food

By this time you should have chosen the soft food you intend using for the coming breeding season, ensuring that you have sufficient time to condition the birds to the new food, if a change from the previous season has been made.

Feed twice a week in small quantities, either in finger drawers for the single cocks or in egg food dishes for the groups of hens, and be sure that all the food is eaten before it goes stale.

Water

Clean water should always be provided, and the

RIGHT: *Chickweed is a favourite green food for canaries, who will often eat it and ignore all other foods. For this reason, when feeding chickweed, always ensure a plentiful supply.*

BELOW: *Young canaries enjoying chickweed off the aviary floor. (Picture courtesy of Mary Holder, Scotland)*

Dandelion has many culinary and medicinal uses. It is a rich source of vitamins A, B complex, C and D, as well as minerals such as iron, potassium, and zinc. All parts are edible, including the root.

supply renewed at least once a day. Never top up stale water, always provide fresh. Bacteria can also build up in the water pipes, so always run the tap for a few moments before collecting fresh water for drinking.

Green foods
Carrot, sprouts, cress, broccoli or wild green foods can all be given in small quantities, as can fresh fruit such as apples and oranges. This need be only once or twice a week, but it all adds to the regular vitamin intake so necessary in the birds' diet.

Supplements
Any supplements used should be provided all year round, regardless of the brands employed. Supplements are just that – they supplement basic feeding, providing the balance of vitamins, proteins and minerals essential for your birds' wellbeing.

Most breeders do supplement their basic

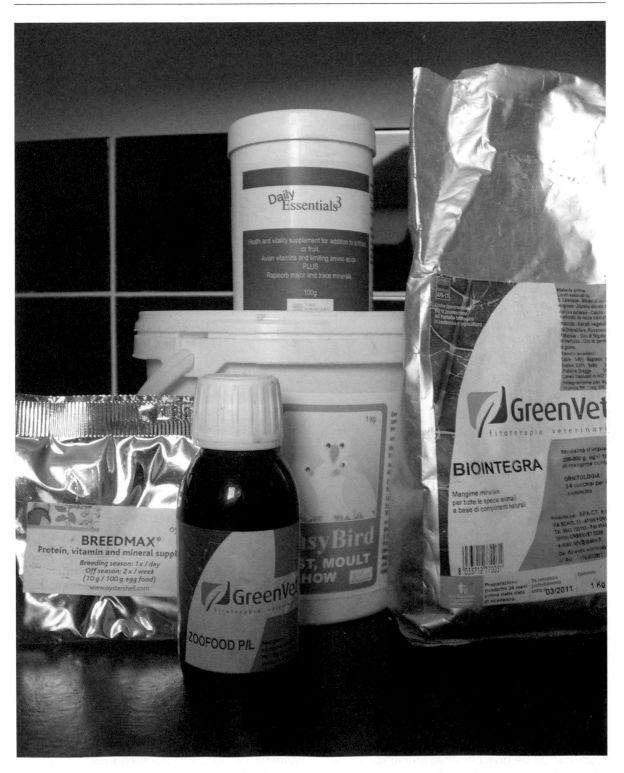

A range of supplements favoured at different times by the author. Care should be taken to feed exactly as the manufacturers' instructions.

feeding in some way, to meet individual needs. Most important from January are calcium, vitamin and protein supplements, given in small quantities only, in addition to the basic feed.

Management
This quarter is the pertinent time to complete various maintenance tasks in the birdroom.

Check your birdroom
Look for leaks, and ensure the room is watertight. Check also that the room is in good general repair, and remains vermin proof. Now is the time to do any repainting, and to complete any necessary building work.

Check your cages
Repair any broken cage fronts, and check that you have enough slides for dividing the cages, and enough wire slides, if these are preferred. Cages should be repainted during this period – you will never have a better chance than at this time of the year when the number of birds to look after is at a minimum.

Also thoroughly clean your show cages and put them away, as they will not be needed until the following October. Keep your training cages available, however, as these will be needed for moving birds about the room in the coming months.

Check your birdroom equipment
Perching, nests, linings, drinkers, seed hoppers, egg food and finger drawers will all be needed in increasing quantity if the breeding season goes according to plan, as well as perhaps feeding trays, cuttlefish bone holders and nesting material racks.

Furthermore it is a good idea to have at least two complete sets of these items, one in use and one clean set always ready for use: this saves hours later on during the breeding season, the busiest time of the year.

Nests and nest linings
January is the time to ensure that nest pans are disinfected and the linings attached, before wrapping them in polythene or plastic bags to keep them clean, and stowing them away; it is also advisable to squirt the bags and nests with an anti-mite preparation.

Breeding register
It is impossible to keep track of even a moderate sized stud without a breeding register. This will keep a record of pairings and the progress they make, and will record the details of the young produced by each pair. Whether you buy in advance of the season, or make your own, being prepared is the order of the day.

Cock birds
Cock birds need to be housed separately. My preference is to use double breeders, which allows them ample exercise to help them develop peak breeding fitness. The brighter days starting in January signal to the cock birds that the breeding season is approaching, and from this time they will be singing lustily until they are paired up.

I also like to house my cock birds in the top row of the cages, as this position allows them maximum daylight, and their song will encourage the hens in their own breeding preparations. I put the cocks I intend running with two or more hens in the top cages, as they are then not alongside any one of their potential partners, and so do not form a pair bond. Furthermore if the breeding hens are not kept in the top cages, it is easier to inspect their nests.

Hens in a flight cage.

Hen birds

Hens are best housed in small groups, about four hens to a triple breeding cage or a small flight cage; this allows them plenty of exercise so they develop good muscle tone over the coming weeks. Do not overcrowd hens, as the weaker ones will risk being pushed back from the feeding stations by the stronger or more adventurous birds.

General Management

The best conditioner at this time is to maintain clean conditions, including access to regular supplies of grits and bath water on clear, dry days.

As regards management tasks during this period, check that the hens' claws do not grow too long, and if they are, trim them so they are not disadvantaged in flight by making perching or landing uncomfortable.

All stock should be dusted with insect powder during mid-February, and again at the end of the month. To do this, hold the bird in one hand over an open sheet of newspaper and shake some powder on to the neck, then gradually work it down the back of the bird. Place some under each wing and on the rump, blowing the feathers around so as to work the powder in. Turn the bird over and repeat the process, working the powder from the breast downwards. It takes only a few seconds to dust each bird, and it can then be returned to its cage. The bird will preen itself, and the next day a bath can be given, to help recondition the feathers. Baths can continue to be given as regularly as is practical.

It is important to repeat this process after ten days, by which time any mite eggs on the bird will have hatched, and the immature mites can be killed before their breeding cycle recommences.

There are several very good pyrethium-based insect powders on the market, including one with an inhibitor which ensures that any insects missed never gain maturity.

Each cage needs to be treated regularly for insects, either by spraying or by washing down with an insecticide. There is little point in cleaning the birds, only for them to be reinfected by dirty surroundings.

Removing stock to breeding cages
Hens can be moved to their respective breeding cages from mid March; each hen should occupy a double breeding cage.

If you intend pair breeding, the cock can be placed in a cage adjacent to the hen, or if you are operating with fewer cocks than hens, then it is best to leave the cocks where they are. Keeping the cocks on the top row means they cannot see the hens and so are unlikely to form pair bonds, which may work against you if it is your intention breed the cock with several different partners.

At this time it is a good idea to trim the vent feathers from the birds, to assist fertilization, especially in birds with softer, longer feathers. Do this with a sharp pair of scissors, though be careful not to remove the guide feathers from either the cocks or the hens. Any feathering removed will regrow at the next moult, in good time for the coming show season.

Lighting
January is the time to decide whether to use artificial lighting to extend the daylight, so giving the birds more hours in which to raise their broods, in the early part of the year. Most fanciers using lights extend the daylight by switching on lighting in the mornings, advancing 'lighting up times' by about fifteen minutes per week, until by early April a day of about fourteen hours is provided. This allows the birds to roost naturally, feeding their young sufficiently to last through a 'shortened' night.

Heating
A constant temperature of around 40–45°F is all that is necessary to maintain the birds' condition during January. This should rise slowly until a constant temperature of 60°F is achieved from April onwards.

Summer (April to June)

Officially summer starts in April, but the canary breeding season starts as soon as the birds tell you they are ready: hens will be seen carrying feathers and wood shavings, flying vertically, constantly calling to the cock birds, and squatting when the cocks sing in response. The cocks will be singing vigorously, pulling themselves to a pencil-thin shape, swaggering up and down the perch with wings dropped, and constantly feeding regurgitated food to their toes, cage front and perch. This behaviour tells you they are ready to breed.

Feeding
Continue feeding as during March, remembering to provide grit and cuttlefish, particularly for the hens, or to give liquid calcium as a supplement if you prefer.

As the hens begin to incubate their eggs they will probably ignore all extra titbits, and exist on a plain seed and water diet as they await hatching time.

Provide soft food from the day before the first chicks hatch; when the chicks hatch, feed fresh soft food, soaked seeds and green food at least twice daily.

Management
As the canary breeding season gets under way, time is at a premium, and this is when an established system will be appreciated.

Cocks should be moved into the hens' cages once each day, and left until mating has been seen to take place; continue this practice until the third egg has been laid. If you are pair breeding, then cocks can be left with the hens, unless they prove to be troublesome, when the best course of action is to house them separately, then to proceed as above.

It is most useful at this time to place a cardboard record card on the outside of the stock cage, on which notes can be written.

Detailed advice on the special requirements of the breeding season is provided in Chapter 5. The main management issues may be summarized as follows:

- Provide adequate nesting material to allow nesting to commence in earnest
- Monitor to ensure fighting does not take place, and remove the cock birds if necessary
- Check nests daily for new eggs
- Remove the first three eggs each day; return when the fourth egg is laid
- Canary eggs take fourteen days to hatch, from the date the eggs are returned
- Remove the cock birds to separate cages whilst the hen incubates the eggs
- Watch for signs of hatching fourteen days after incubation commences
- Return the cock bird to help feed the chicks from the third day, and monitor carefully
- Check the cage floor regularly for chicks that have fallen from the nest
- Provide fresh soft food two or more times each day, for the newly hatched chicks
- Feed soaked seeds daily from the third day after hatching
- Feed green food daily from the third day after hatching
- Remove any uneaten/stale food from the cage floor every day
- Apply closed rings when the birds are four to seven days old
- Check the nest pans for mite, and replace with a new nest after the chicks are ten days old

- Provide a second nest at the opposite end of the cage when the chicks are fifteen days old
- Provide new nesting material to prevent the chicks being plucked
- Monitor egg-laying activities as described earlier, and repeat the management routine

Autumn (July to September)

July marks the end of the breeding season and the start of the annual moult, which continues until September, or in some cases even later. Replacing their plumage is often taxing for canaries, and every care should be taken to help them come through this period as quickly as possible, particularly the adult birds after the rigorous demands of the breeding season.

The moult is a quiet time in the canary calendar, and the same management regime applies throughout the whole period. The following is a summary of their needs:

- Fresh water: daily
- Mixed canary seed: daily
- Condition seed: once a week
- Soft food: daily
- Colour food: daily
- Greenfoods/fruits: twice a week
- Minerals: mineral grit, oystershell grit, charcoal, cuttlefish: always available
- Supplements: as recommended by the manufacturer
- Housing: adult birds in flight cages, young birds a single bird per cage
- Bathing: twice a week
- Heating: maintain a constant temperature of 45–55°F
- Lighting: no artificial lighting required
- Show training: allow young birds to use the training cages daily, until deep in moult

Canaries benefit from exercise in flight cages or from small indoor or outdoor aviaries, with protective roofs. Here, a millet spray provides a tasty treat. (Picture courtesy of Mary Holder, Scotland)

Winter (October to December)

October marks the end of the moult for most canaries, and the start of the exhibition season, which lasts until December. This is officially the resting period for our canaries, but it is also the most sociable time of the canary enthusiast's year, as they have the opportunity to meet many fellow hobbyists at the various exhibitions, both at home and overseas, and exchange breeding stories, birds, or both!

At the end of the year, fanciers begin to prepare their birds for their natural breeding cycle, which begins each year in spring.

Feeding and management are reduced to minimum levels, to reflect the reduced needs of the birds during the resting period. The following is a summary of their needs:

- Fresh water: daily
- Mixed canary seed: daily
- Condition seed: once a week
- Soft food: once a week
- Green foods/fruits: once a week
- Minerals: provide mineral grit, oystershell grit, charcoal and cuttlefish at all times
- Supplements: feed as recommended by the manufacturer
- Housing: exhibition birds – a single bird per cage; stock birds – small groups in the flight cages
- Bathing: weekly
- Heating: no artificial heating is required
- Lighting: no artificial lighting is required

5 Breeding Canaries

Breeding canaries is a fascinating and rewarding hobby which can be enjoyed by all age groups from school children upwards, including those who are retired. It is extremely absorbing – better still, it is a year-round task, and is not weather-dependent. Given average conditions and management, canaries will breed freely, producing and raising an average yield of chicks every year. To breed a given number of birds you can therefore generally achieve your aims using a basic formula.

Canary hens will produce a minimum of two nests of eggs each breeding season.

These are called clutches, and contain an average of four eggs per clutch. In the UK canary breeders generally breed from approximately sixteen hen canaries, and these hens will produce between them thirty-two clutches of eggs, resulting in 128 eggs each year. Success lies in maximizing the chances of these eggs being fertile, and then being successfully incubated and reared to maturity. If 50 per cent of the eggs are fertile, this will result in sixty-four 'full' eggs. A 50 per cent hatch will result in thirty-two new-born chicks, and if 50 per cent of these

are raised, then you will have sixteen fledged canaries (one per hen).

The key to producing larger numbers of canaries per year lies in increasing the average yield per hen, from one raised chick each up to four or more. Most breeders of the larger varieties of canary recognize that an average return of forty chicks from sixteen hens (2.5 chicks per hen) represents a successful breeding season. Smaller canary varieties are more productive, and will return four or more chicks per hen on average.

This means that a stud of Norwich, Yorkshire or Border canaries consisting of twelve cock birds and sixteen hens, will, with only average success, increase in number to a total of forty-four birds (adults plus their young); increasing the average yield should produce an end number of sixty-eight birds in your birdroom at the end of the breeding season. Repeat the formula with an equal breeding team of Fifes or Lizard canaries for example, and you will be looking for cage room to accommodate a total of ninety-two canaries, at least until after the moult has been completed!

Achieving these increased breeding returns will turn a season of average success into an exceptional one, which is every canary breeder's aim each year.

THE ANNUAL CYCLE

As mentioned initially, keeping canaries is a year-round hobby. The year is divided into seasons, and these are cyclic, corresponding to the climate.

In general in the UK, canaries breed between April and June: this is known as the 'breeding season'. Conditioning canaries for the breeding season is a process that cannot be rushed, and it takes time and planning to accomplish the required body changes and general condition. In my opinion planning for a successful breeding season commences with the annual moult, which in effect means that we are planning for next season immediately the current breeding season has come to an end.

Canaries in the UK will start their annual moult in July. Ideally this process is completed quickly, and should be as relatively stress free for the birds as possible. This is especially true for adult hen canaries, which will have had a hectic three months or so already, producing and rearing their chicks. This is taxing on their health, especially if the breeding season has been prolonged. Rather than using individual cages, I prefer to moult my hen canaries in small groups in flight cages, where they can enjoy increased exercise and freedom. I find they generally moult more quickly this way, which is the ultimate aim.

When considering which birds to retain for the following year's breeding programme the first point of attention should not concern their exhibition qualities, but their general health and condition as they emerge from their moult. In six short months the breeding cycle will begin again, and the fancier does not need any passengers, no matter how fine their exhibition points!

The UK show season, generally from October to January, is actually nature's resting period, and is necessary in order for the birds to regain their vigour. Not only have they come through a taxing breeding season, they have also achieved a complete makeover, moulting out and regrowing their entire plumage. They deserve a few months rest. Of course, exhibition strains of canary have been bred to enjoy taking part in a relatively busy show season during this same period, but it is not surprising if sometimes the adult birds

Good management is key to raising young canaries to maturity. (Picture courtesy of George Ioannides, Cyprus)

appear to be less than enthusiastic about this! It is therefore important not to over-show your adult birds, especially those which may be forming the nucleus of your future breeding programme. It is good policy to let them rest, to feed them well, and to wait for spring.

The final quarter of the year, from January to March, is known collectively as the 'preparation period' for the upcoming breeding season. During this period the fancier will be exercising his stock, increasing the richness of the daily and weekly feeding programme, and perhaps adjusting the heating and lighting used in the birdroom in order to maximize the canaries' fitness in anticipation of the beginning of the breeding season.

The four seasons of the canary year in fact directly concur with nature, as they mimic the conditions that wild finches face throughout the year. Finches breed when it is warm and food is plentiful, after which they moult, then they recuperate and store food and energy during the long dark winter months, before finally emerging in the spring, making preparations for the new breeding season. Thus the breeding season is actually a year-round task and not just a three-month wonder, and similarly, managing our canaries through the year successfully will greatly influence our success or failure rate during the breeding cycle itself. Thus it is essential that only the fitter, more active hens are retained for breeding, that they are nurtured correctly and exercised throughout the year, and in short, are prepared for the taxing breeding season ahead.

If the cock birds are cared for in the same way, then an increase in fertile eggs will also be achieved – if this figure can be raised to 75 per cent, then the average yield of full eggs will increase from sixty-four (representing 50 per cent fertility) to ninety-six fertile eggs. Even using 'bottom line' figures for a bad year, this equates to twenty-four chicks raised instead of only sixteen.

THE BREEDING CYCLE

Canaries are finches and their breeding cycle

The instinct to breed is strong in canaries generally. Here two red canaries tend their chicks. (Picture courtesy of Panos Paniagotides, Greece)

is the same as that of our native finches, so observing native finches, their activities, the foods they eat and the timing of their own nesting, will greatly assist anyone new to canary breeding as a hobby. During the breeding season, native finches will choose a partner and act territorially, defending their partner and their home and its surrounding territory against intruders. Canaries often have their partners chosen for them by the fancier and are placed into individual breeding cages, and from here, a pair bond develops, again mimicking nature.

Finches produce a first nest of young generally in April or May, and follow this by raising a second brood. If things go wrong or perhaps if predators intervene, the finches will often move home, then immediately produce a replacement nest, followed by a third. Overall, finches appear to be driven to produce a certain number of chicks to ensure the survival of their family line, given that the percentage of fledglings actually making it through to maturity is relatively low in the wild. This is a factor which canary breeders can use to their distinct advantage.

Breeding Methodologies

The majority of exhibition canaries bred in the UK each year are produced using a system known as pair breeding. This follows nature's way most closely, as outlined above, and has the distinct advantage of both parents being on hand to help rear the chicks.

An alternative methodology is to 'run' the cock bird, when the better cock canaries are mated to more than one hen in order to fertilize eggs with multiple partners. Both methodologies are discussed in detail below.

Whilst it is general practice for successful canary hens to rear two broods in the UK, it is also true that they will produce more eggs if their first clutch is unsuccessful, just as finches do. Using this knowledge, regardless of which breeding methods are used, canary fanciers can increase the yield of eggs per hen from an average of eight eggs (two nests of four eggs each), to twelve eggs (three nests of four eggs), with no ill effect upon the hen.

This increased yield of fertile eggs completely transcends our original average yield. With proper year-round management the original sixty-four fertile eggs became ninety-six, and this has increased significantly to 144 fertile eggs, resulting in a minimum return of thirty-six chicks being raised to maturity, against our original forecast of just sixteen chicks.

BREEDING SYSTEMS EXPLAINED

Worldwide there are several methodologies used to produce canaries. Understanding each system may help newcomers to produce more canaries to meet their individual requirements. Many established fanciers practise several different breeding methodologies simultaneously, in order to achieve their particular objectives.

Pair Breeding

In pair breeding, fanciers will pair one cock with one hen bird, so they form a bond for the entire breeding period. Fanciers sometimes leave the cock and hen bird together in the same cage throughout the breeding season; others prefer to remove the cock bird to a separate cage, when the hen is incubating her eggs. Once the eggs have hatched, the cock may be reintroduced into the hen's cage so he can help rear the young. Much will depend on the temperament of the cock bird, and the behaviour of each individual bird needs to be carefully monitored to ensure accidents do not happen.

The advantage of pair breeding is that a larger number of chicks are generally reared than by other breeding methods. All will be full brothers and sisters, whether they hatched in the first, second or even the third nest of the year. This provides a wide range of choice for those people who are confident of the pair's abilities and qualities.

Running a Cock Bird

Fanciers sometimes choose to pair their best cock birds with several hens during a single breeding season. This is known as 'running' the cock bird, which is housed separately, and only introduced to the hen for the purpose of mating.

Once a successful mating has occurred, the cock is returned to his own quarters, before being introduced to a second or subsequent hen, and the process is then repeated. This procedure is generally repeated until the second or third egg has been laid, when the hen is left to complete her clutch without the attentions of the cock bird.

Fanciers using the above method generally do not allow the cock bird to rear any young chicks with any of his 'wives', as they do not wish a pair bond to form. This could impact upon the cock bird's interests in mating with other hens, to the detriment of the breeding programme.

The advantage of running cock birds is that significant numbers of related birds can be produced, which may then be interbred in order to develop a breeding line centred around one original bird.

Colony Breeding

People who keep birds simply for pleasure often favour colony breeding. A colony generally comprises a limited number of cock birds and several more hen birds, which live together harmoniously in a large aviary throughout the

year. Multiple nesting sites are established, and the birds simply 'get on with it' themselves, without interference from the bird keeper.

Care should be taken not to overcrowd the colony, otherwise the territorial instincts of the birds will be provoked during the breeding season and fighting may occur, causing possible fatalities, and certainly impacting upon the successful production of young birds.

A second important consideration is the feather quality of the birds used in the breeding programme. It is far safer to keep all buff cock birds and yellow hen birds for example, as that way the established practice of pairing buff feather to yellow feather will be maintained throughout the colony.

Line Breeding

Line breeding is the system of pairing together birds that are descended from related bloodlines. Common pairings include cousin x cousin, grandfather x granddaughter, and so on. By using related birds, fanciers are better able to control the gene pool within their stud, to help produce more birds possessing specific qualities – for example type, style, head or feather qualities.

In-breeding

In-breeding is a concentrated form of line breeding, involving the use of much more closely related pairings: father x daughter, mother x son and even brother x sister pairings are frequently used. The aims of both line breeding and in-breeding is to establish, as far as possible, a genetic purity amongst the stock to help guarantee more accurately the qualities of the young birds produced.

Those who breed pedigree studs of birds generally practise some form of line breeding in order to control more closely the inheritance of preferred attributes of their stock, by seeking to maintain genetic purity as outlined above.

In simplistic terms, pairing two unrelated birds together will produce offspring carrying 50 per cent of the father's genes and 50 per cent of the mother's genes. At this stage, neither parent may be dominant to the other, and the outcome from this pairing owes as much to luck as to any other factor. However, if the resultant chick is matched back to either the father or the mother, then the resultant offspring will be carrying 75 per cent of the original parent's genes, with only 25 per cent influence from the second original grandparent. This means that the chicks will more closely resemble their father or their mother (whichever was used in the second pairing), and in any future matings will be more likely to breed true to the qualities possessed by that particular bird.

By continually pairing related birds in the same line, a family of birds which closely resemble each other can be produced over time, which will in turn produce consistent quality amongst their offspring. New blood needs to be introduced into the line periodically to ensure that vigour is maintained, or to improve any qualities which may be lacking; but these general principles remain true for all types of pedigree livestock.

Outcrosses

An outcross refers to a bird carrying an unrelated blood line, which is different from the original stock. Outcrosses are used to ensure improved 'hybrid vigour', or to introduce characteristics lacking in the original stock.

BREEDING SEASON EVENTS

Typical breeding season events can be summarized as follows:

- Preparing the birds
- Introducing the nest
- Introducing the cock
- The first egg
- Incubation
- Hatching
- Rearing
- Weaning
- Second round

Preparing the Birds

Birds should be prepared for breeding from January onwards. Follow a fitness routine for both cocks and hens, using flight cages or inside aviaries to maximize the amount of exercise potential for your stock. After the quiet winter period and the end of the show season, your birds will enjoy the increasing daylight hours that January brings. Lighting can be artificially increased to bring forward the actual onset of breeding. Concentrate on bringing your birds into breeding condition gradually, over a defined period.

Initially both cock and hen birds can be housed in flights or aviary together, although a watchful eye should be kept for potential troublemakers. Fighting will occur if the birds are overcrowded, or if insufficient feeding stations are provided.

Remember, too, that if using an inside aviary for the first time, perching should be available low down initially, until the birds have gained some muscle tone; it can be moved gradually to higher levels as the birds' fitness improves, and to encourage as much vertical flying as possible.

Also, gradually increase the supplies of food that you intend offering the birds when they are rearing young, so they become accustomed to the taste.

By the end of February you will need to remove the cock canaries from the flights to avoid fighting and to ensure that pair bonds do not form. A couple of weeks later, remove the

Initially during the preparation period, both cocks and hens can share the same flight accommodation.

Shrubs are attractive in an aviary, but are not immune from attack by canaries. Placed in containers, shrubs can be removed and allowed to recover before too much damage is done. (Picture courtesy of Mary Holder, Scotland)

The hen has built her nest and the cock bird sings joyously. Eggs will appear any day now.

hens and place them into their own individual double breeding cages.

At this stage each bird should be examined for mite, at the same time checking bodyweight and fat residues, and the condition of beak and claws. Any birds that still have a layer of yellowish fat around the abdomen will benefit from another two weeks in the aviary or flight cage, because obese birds do not lay eggs! Ideally the hen canaries should have a plump, rounded abdomen and an abundance of soft downy feathering, indicating peak condition. Cock birds will be slimmer, with a protruding vent.

At this stage, claws should be trimmed to ensure they are not overlong, which could result in damage to the bird, the eggs or to any young chicks, and in extreme cases may result in infertile eggs. Clipping nails is a task that most people can achieve with little difficulty. Hold the bird allowing one claw to wrap around your finger as you curl your hand around the body of the bird. This gives the canary a sense of security. The head should pop out above your thumb and first finger, with the tail pointing down your wrist. Turning your hand over, lift out one leg, and extend the claws.

Generally it is just the hind claw and the middle front-facing claw that will need attention. Use a small pair of specially designed nail clippers with curved jaws which can be operated with one hand. Hold the extended claw up to the light, and a single vein will be seen running through the centre of the nail. Clip near to this vein, but be careful not to cut it as you do not want the canary to suffer any loss of blood. If an accident happens, a dab of iodine usually works, or in a severe case cauterize the end of the nail with a lit cigarette, taper or smouldering match to prevent the loss of blood.

Sometimes the beak also grows too long. Whilst you have the bird in your hand, place your thumb gently on the bird's head and assess how the beak is aligned. The lower and upper mandibles should meet each other,

enabling the bird to feed with ease. If not, snip off the excess using the nail clippers: keep your thumb or finger on top of the bird's head to ensure its beak is closed to avoid accidentally nicking its tongue.

Whilst holding the canary, check the condition of the legs, and consider whether it would benefit from having horns or scales reduced. If so, massage some olive oil or a proprietary solution on to the leg for a few days, which will have the effect of softening and reducing the worst scales. Delay introduction into the flight until this operation has been completed.

To reduce stress caused by handling the bird too frequently, it is wise to trim away any excess vent feathering and to add mite powder before

A Lancashire Canary hen with her chick. The nest is positioned close to a perch, to allow easy access by the parent birds. (Picture courtesy of Panos Paniagotides, Greece)

releasing it into the breeding cage. Trimming the excess vent feathers will aid successful mating. This practice is generally not necessary with smaller, shorter-feathered canaries, but larger canary breeds will all benefit from a trim. Hold the bird securely in one hand, then place the scissors across the belly and make a cut straight across the feathers above the vent. From this cut, snip down each flank, removing the excess feathering around the vent. Hold the bird's legs and feet securely out of range of the scissors, to avoid accidents.

Be careful to leave intact the ring of guide feathers immediately around the vent. These feathers aid mating, and should remain in place at all times.

Apply a dusting of anti-mite powder to the trimmed bird before placing it into its breeding cage. Trimmed feathers will regrow when your canary completes its annual moult from July onwards. Both cocks and hens should be trimmed.

At some stage during this preparation period it is also important to check the condition of the cages, and to ensure that you have adequate supplies of nest pans, liners, nesting material, dummy eggs, soft food containers and all the various breeding foods that will be required throughout the breeding season.

Otherwise keep a check on your garden, taking note of how the plants are blossoming and the activities of the native birds: when they breed, generally speaking, so can your canaries.

Introducing the Nest

Nest pans should be placed in position in the hen's cage approximately two weeks before you anticipate that she will lay her first egg. They can be hung directly on the cage wall, or placed on top of weighted plant pots, even hung outside the cage in a wire container. Perching should be available, placed about half an inch below the lip of the nest: this helps to ensure that the hen hops on to the perch rather than flies straight off the nest, which could dislodge any newly hatched chicks out of the nest to perish.

Most fanciers use plastic nest pans, although earthenware bowls or purpose-built wooden nest pans are still used successfully by more traditional breeders. Wicker baskets are also sometimes used. Earthenware bowls offer a

An inspection door allows easy access to the nest for the owner. (Picture courtesy of F. and M. Haerens, Belgium)

Prior to breeding, nest felts are glued into position using carbolic soap.

larger nesting facility and may therefore favour the larger breeds; they also are less subject to temperature changes, and can be soaked to provide a moist atmosphere and aid hatching, which is especially beneficial in warmer weather.

Nest linings are generally felt or jute, and can be glued or stitched into place through the ventilation holes of the nest pan. Some older fanciers melt carbolic soap and use this to secure the nest lining in position, as it was believed that the aroma from the soap deterred mite. Modern fanciers use proprietary adhesives or wallpaper paste, which is extremely effective. Soaking the nest lining itself in a solution containing a mite repellent is certainly worthwhile, as mite are the single most common reason for failing to rear chicks.

When introducing the nest, also provide a quantity of nesting material, such as jute, string, hessian sacking, etc. Avoid cotton or lengths of wool as these materials can become entangled around the birds' claws, causing damage. Most avian suppliers offer competitively priced nest-building materials. When the hen is seen nest-building in earnest, it is safe to introduce the cock bird: if you are using the traditional pair breeding method, the cock can remain with the hen throughout the breeding season.

Introducing the Cock

As explained above, there are generally two methods of breeding exhibition canaries: pair breeding, where one cock bird is mated to a single hen, or running the cock bird to multiple hens. Fanciers with high demands on their available free time, or who are relatively inexperienced, are advised to use pair breeding as their preferred method, whilst those with more experience may prefer to run their cock birds, or use a mixture of both breeding methods throughout the season. In terms of producing large numbers of canaries, pair breeding is by far the most successful method. Pair breeding mirrors nature by allowing a bond to develop between the birds, and they will then share the responsibility of raising their family.

Running the cock bird to several hens removes both these options, and introduces an element of timing into the equation in order for the second round of eggs to be fertilized. It does, however, enable the physically superior exhibition specimens to be mated to more females, and hence to pass on their genetic characteristics to as much of the stud as possible, more efficiently.

The down side to pair breeding is that the lesser cock birds are impacting the development of the stud; also the fancier must make ideal partner selections if progress in the stud is to be maintained.

Traditionally fanciers use the double breeding cage when breeding: the hen is placed in one compartment, whilst their intended mate is housed in the second compartment, with the slide dividing the cage withdrawn a fraction so the birds can become acquainted. Alternatives are a slide with circular holes, or an all-wire divider, through which the two birds become accustomed to each other. This method is advantageous when pair breeding because a bond can be encouraged, and it enables the safe introduction of the male when the hen begins to show an interest in nesting.

For breeders intending to run the cock bird between partners the above method is unsuitable. Hens breeding in this way should be allowed to build their nests unaided, and the cock birds kept out of sight of their partners. The cock bird is run into a training cage (generally an old show cage), which is then hung on the breeding cage of the intended partner, at which point the cock bird will generally sing vigorously. When the hen squats and flutters her wings, lifting her tail, this is a sure sign that she has accepted the cock bird, and he can be placed in her breeding cage. Mating will generally follow immediately, when the cock can be removed in the training cage and returned to his own stock cage.

The above practice is continued twice daily until the completion of the clutch of eggs, at which point the cock's breeding duties with that particular hen are over. She will now incubate and rear her chicks on her own.

The First Egg

Nesting canary hens will generally lay eggs within ten days from completing their nest. The fertilization of a clutch of eggs is assumed to take place at a single mating, which should occur a few days before the egg is produced. When pair breeding, this poses no problems, but when running cock birds it is crucial to recognize the condition of the hen and her nesting progress. This is why fanciers introduce their chosen cock birds daily, and continue to do so until the clutch has been completed, even if biologically this may not be necessary.

The following signs will indicate that the hen is ready to lay her eggs: her body shape will change and become rounder, she will spend more time sitting in the nest, and will drink a great deal of water in comparison to the usual amount she consumes.

Eggs from each nest are stored in a single compartment, numbered with the cage number, to avoid any mistakes.

Dummy plastic eggs are used to temporarily replace the genuine eggs, until the full clutch has been laid.

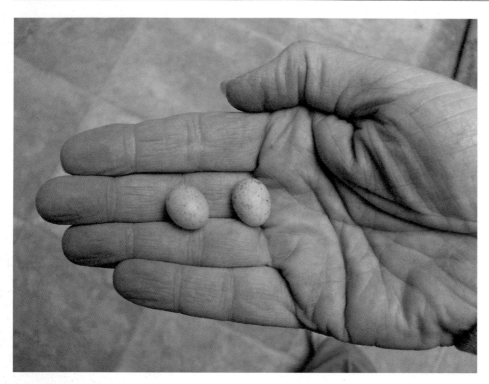

The difference beween fake and genuine eggs is overlooked by canary hens.

Eggs returned to a well-constructed nest. The eggs are placed on a coating of anti-mite powder, which helps to deter these unwanted pests.

Canary hens incubating eggs are very reluctant to leave them unattended.

It is common practice to remove each egg on the morning it is laid, replacing it with a plastic dummy egg. The real eggs are stored on a bed of seed, sawdust or nesting felt, and are turned each day until the clutch of eggs is complete, when all are replaced under the hen. This is done to ensure that all eggs hatch within a few hours of each other, giving each chick an equal chance of survival.

Incubation

Canary eggs take on average thirteen and a half days to hatch, from the point when incubation commences. In the case of the wild finch, the hen rarely incubates her eggs until the clutch is complete: she is away foraging for food and making final touches to her nest. Domesticated canaries, on the other hand, have nowhere to go and nothing to do because their every need is catered for, and so they often commence incubating as soon as they lay their first egg. This egg would therefore hatch three, four or five days before the last egg laid, giving the later chick a very poor chance of survival.

This is why the eggs are removed, and only returned to the nest once the last egg has been laid. The last egg will generally be a slightly different colour shade than the first eggs, however many eggs the hen lays per clutch. The average is four eggs per nest, but this will vary, depending largely upon the age and fitness of the hen.

Eggs can be retained for several days before being returned to the nest. This practice is also

BREEDING RECORD CARDS

Simple cardboard record cards can be hung on canary breeding cages to provide privacy for nesting canaries.

They are convenient places to record the daily activities of the birds during this busy period, and the details can later be transferred into a stud book for a more permanent record.

Round number	*1*	Cage number	*16*
Cock	*09 buff red ring*	Hen	*09 clear yellow ring no. 21*

Date paired	*4 April 2012*
1st egg laid	*10.4.2012*
2nd egg laid	*11.4.2012*
3rd egg laid	*12.4.2012*
4th egg laid	*13.4.2012*
Date eggs set	*pm 12.4.2012*
Date due to hatch	*26.4.2012*
Results	*4 hatched 26 April*
	Both parents feeding well
	Hen plucking chicks after 17 days
	New nest and material provided
Chicks left the nest	*16 May 2012*
Ring details	*orange rings, nos 4, 5, 6, 7*
Date weaned	*21 May 2012*

helpful if two hens have commenced laying, but one is a day or two adrift of the other. No harm will come to any eggs retained, and the advantage of returning the eggs to both hens at the same time is that both nests should then hatch within hours of each other, providing a convenient foster mother, if needed.

It is a good idea when replacing the eggs to ensure the nest has been constructed solidly, with a firm bottom surface so the hen can turn her eggs constantly and successfully throughout incubation. This helps to prevent the condition known as 'dead in shell', when full eggs can be lost prematurely, for no apparent reason. A soft surface in the nest can prevent the hen from turning the eggs during incubation. Pressing a small ball or light bulb into the bottom of the nest before returning it to the hen helps to compress the construction, which will aid successful incubation. Also take the opportunity

OPPOSITE: **Newly hatched chicks, which are born blind, without feathers. The moist covering soon dries after hatching.**

to sprinkle mite powder into the nest before placing the eggs inside and returning the nest to the waiting hen.

It is most important to allow the birds privacy in order to raise their family undisturbed. Hanging a small card on the cage wires to shield the nest from view will serve the dual purpose of providing privacy and also a place to make notes, such as when the eggs are due to hatch, and the events from that point forwards.

Cock birds will often try to assist with incubation, protecting the eggs whilst the hen is feeding until she returns to the nest and recommences her duties. Beware, however, the cock which tries to roost alongside the hen, or which sits abreast on the nest, because he is

endangering the clutch, both from breakage, and more importantly because he is preventing incubation, as he lacks the hen's brood spot which is necessary to bring the eggs to the point of hatching.

In these circumstances the only option is to remove the cock bird to his own side of the double breeding cage, separated by the dividing slide. If the hen canary persists in visiting the cock bird, leaving her eggs to do so, then remove the cock to another cage totally out of view of the hen.

Generally speaking, hens that have incubated for several days will not be tempted off the nest by the removal of the cock bird, but those sitting for less time may become flighty or

may even desert their eggs. You will have two choices at this point: either to return the cock and trust to luck, or to foster the eggs (having marked them) by putting them into another nest, and starting all over again.

Sometimes hens will desert their eggs for no apparent reason. Usually this occurs with unflighted hens that simply want to 'go again', and fostering the eggs is the only solution. This is particularly vexing when the hen has sat for ten or twelve days perfectly well, then jumps off the nest for no reason.

Hatching

Canary eggs hatch approximately fourteen days from when incubation starts. In canary terms, this means from the date 'set' – that is, when the eggs have been returned to the nest. Successful hatching is dependent upon each hen incubating correctly, for the required amount of time, combined with a reasonable ambient temperature being maintained within the birdroom – 60°F is generally considered to be ideal. This can be maintained by providing birdroom heating attached to thermometers, particularly during the earlier part of the breeding season when weather conditions are unstable.

A day or so before hatching, eggs should be dampened with water in order to increase the immediate humidity and assist the hatching process by enabling the chick to break through the shell more easily. Canary eggs are porous but can be floated in warm water: full eggs will bob up and down, whilst clear or 'dead in shell' eggs will simply float motionless on the surface. An alternative to floating eggs is to spray them with tepid water when the hen moves from the nest to feed.

Canary chicks are equipped with a solitary egg tooth, which erodes as they chip through the shell. The hen will assist them to hatch, but care should always be taken that egg shells do not completely dry out, as this will generally impede the hatching process, or stop it all together. If this is noticed, apply water with a small paintbrush, then allow nature to take its course.

Despite removing the eggs, it is common for a single chick to hatch up to a day behind its siblings. This difference can usually be caught up during the rearing process, but if the smaller chick falls behind its nestlings then it should be removed to a nest containing smaller chicks, to give it a better chance of survival.

Rearing

It is important not to disturb your canaries immediately they have hatched. Their mother and father will be most protective, and almost secretive about their charges, and the only evidence that you have new hatchlings will be broken eggshells hidden in the far corner of the cage, and a plaintive cheeping from the nest.

Rather than disturb the parents, I find that by providing a small titbit and retiring from the birdroom, the parent will be enticed off the nest after a few short minutes. Pop back after five minutes and you may just get a quick look during which you can check that all is well.

Don't worry if you don't see the parents feeding the chicks in the first instance. The yolk sac from the egg has been absorbed into the chick's body and will sustain it for the first twenty-four hours. After that time, the hen will have become accustomed to her new parental status, and will begin feeding them.

Allow the birds enough privacy to raise their families undisturbed, supported by regular small supplies of food.

Initially all that is required is soft food, which will need replacing regularly; after three days support this with offerings of soaked seed and green food, in addition to the usual seed and water. (See Chapter 4 for how to prepare both soft food and soaked or sprouted seeds.)

Chicks at four days old. The growth rate of young birds is rapid. (Picture courtesy of Panos Paniagotides, Greece)

Chicks at six days old. The growth rate of these young birds continues to increase rapidly. (Picture courtesy of George Ioannides, Cyprus)

Chicks at one week old. Notice that their eyes are not yet open. (Picture courtesy of Panos Paniagotides, Greece)

Occasionally, canary hens are not good mothers. Chicks can be hand fed if necessary, using a moist rearing mixture. (Picture courtesy of Panos Paniagotides, Greece)

Chicks at ten days old. Now the feather colouration can be clearly seen.

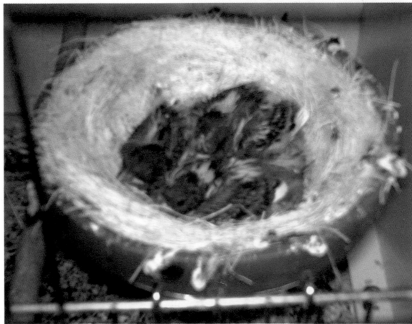

These chicks are growing rapidly and feathering well. (Picture courtesy of F. and M. Haerens, Belgium)

APPLYING A CLOSED RING TO A CANARY

To apply a closed ring, gather the three forward-pointing toes together and insert into the ring. Gently slide the ring up the leg, covering the rear toe and claw, until the claw is finally released.

Closed rings of the correct size can only be applied to young birds up to about seven days of age, when the feet and toes are still very supple.

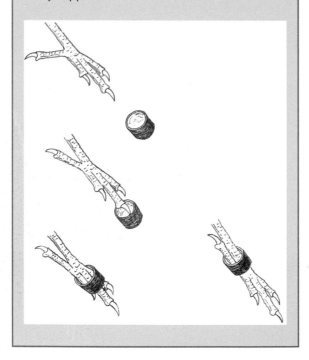

Canary chicks are born without feathers and are blind, their eyes appearing as two large round bulges on the side of their head. They will be covered in down, but are otherwise bald. Feathers begin to grow as they mature, and by the time they are ten days old they will be feathered to the extent that you can determine their colour and the amount of variegation.

After a few days the chick's eyes will begin to open, and they will grow rapidly.

Depending on the variety of canary, it may or may not require ringing for exhibition. If it requires a closed ring, this should be applied when the chick is between four and seven days old, depending upon the rate of growth. If you miss the latter date, do not try to force the ring on to the bird as you risk damaging the hind toe and claw, which will make the bird lame. Similarly, after applying leg rings, always check the next day to ensure none has slipped off, because it is possible that they can be reapplied at that early stage.

Identifying canaries is made easier by the practice of ringing. Split rings are used by many breeders in preference to closed rings, as they are easy to apply, readily available and relatively inexpensive. Ringing is best carried out when the young birds are weaned, immediately they are removed from their parents. Ring manufacturers supply a special aluminium tool which stretches a ring open so that it can be applied to the young bird's leg. This is easy to do: hold the bird in one hand, and the chosen leg can easily be laid into the furrow of the ringing tool, and the open ring simply slid down the tool on to the leg in a matter of seconds. A gentle squeeze on the sides of the ring will close it, and the job is done!

One advantage of using a split ring as compared to a closed ring is that the ring can easily be removed should the need arise: simply place the ring applicator alongside the leg, and slide the ring up and off the leg.

If I see young birds pecking or nibbling at their rings I always remove them immediately to prevent them damaging their tender young legs.

I always provide a new, clean nest when the chicks are approximately ten days old. At this stage they will have started voiding over the sides of the nest, and the hen will have stopped removing the faeces sacs. A clean nest provides the growing chicks with more space, and also any mites will be destroyed along with the old nest.

Chicks calling to be fed. Notice the deep red, healthy gapes to attract the parents attention. (Picture courtesy of George Ioannides, Cyprus)

Clean babies in a dirty nest. After a week, canary chicks excrete over the side of the nest, but sometimes they miss!

Sixteen days old and fully feathered. Any sudden scares and these chicks will leave the nest.

The nest is placed on the cage floor, so it is easier to find at night time, to roost.

*This chick
has now left
the nest.*

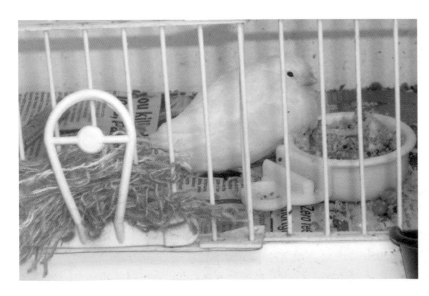

*This chick has now left home
and has just discovered soft food
for the very first time. Note the
nesting material on hand as mum
sets about laying another nest of
eggs.*

With moderate feeding, after eighteen to twenty-one days the chicks will be seen balancing on the side of the nest, ready to take their leave. At this stage another new nest pan should be provided, with ample supplies of nesting material – otherwise the hen may start to pluck her first young in order to build her second nest.

Weaning

Weaning canaries can be a worrying time, but my advice is not to be hasty: wait until you are certain that the chicks are feeding themselves before removing them from their parents. This process usually takes place between twenty-one to twenty-eight days from hatching. Even so, any chicks crying for food should either be returned to their parents, placed in a nursery cage attached to the front of the parents' cage, or housed in the second compartment of the double breeding cage, separated by a wire slide. A few more days of tender parental care, whilst at the same time removing the fledglings from the activities of the nesting hen, will save the chicks and allow their mother to continue her nesting duties relatively undisturbed.

Young canaries soon ready for the big wide world. (Picture courtesy of George Ioannides, Cyprus)

In nest feather, Red Mosaic canaries are a salmon pink colour throughout. It is only when they moult that they gain the distinctive mosaic plumage pattern. (Picture courtesy of Spiros Papirrazos, Greece)

Another young canary ready to be weaned. (Picture courtesy of Panos Paniagotides, Greece)

At only twenty days old, young canaries are often finger tame. (Picture courtesy of George Ioannides, Cyprus)

These chicks are nearly ready to fledge. Note the crest forming on the young chick in the nest. This bird will develop into an exhibition Gloster Corona canary. (Picture courtesy of George Ioannides, Cyprus)

This young canary has just left home. (Picture courtesy of George Ioannides, Cyprus)

As soon as they are feeding themselves, young canaries are kept in groups in the weaning cage, awaiting the onset of the annual moult. (Picture courtesy of F. and M. Haerens, Belgium)

The more canaries you have, the more cages you need! (Picture courtesy of Martin Wright, England)

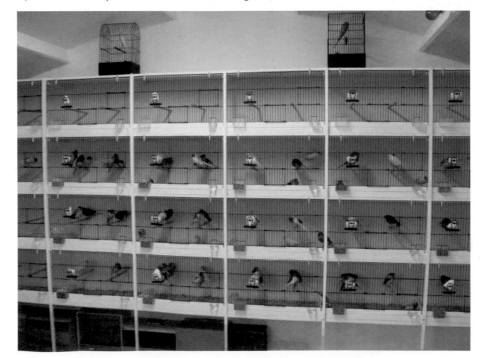

Young canaries will often pick at soil searching out insects and other nutrients. (Picture courtesy of Mary Holder, Scotland)

The canary weaning cage is simply a breeding cage with the perches removed, and paper sheets placed on the cage floor. The sheets can be changed at each feed, removing any spilled soft food which may otherwise turn sour and cause stomach problems. My preference is in fact to provide three perches approximately three inches off the floor and two or three inches apart, at one end of the cage. This has the advantage of teaching the young birds to perch, without them having to fly from one end of the cage to the other, which would risk them landing heavily and damaging their tender young feet.

I also try to wean chicks in groups of perhaps five or six, as they will copy each other and learn quickly. This is particularly useful if any are slow to pick up feed, or when providing shallow baths for the first time.

Before weaning, the chicks will have spent up to four weeks occupying a small nest, where they will have been a target for mite attacks. When they are removed from their parents and placed in new quarters it is a good opportunity to apply a proprietary mite treatment such as Ivermec, or an anti-mite powder, to ensure they do not cross infect each other, and help to repel any unwanted guests.

Similarly, if the chicks have not been fitted with closed rings, this is an ideal time to apply split rings, ensuring easy identification from that point forward.

The chicks should not be given hard seeds at this stage, as they are indigestible to such young birds and may cause the condition known as 'going light' – a wasting disease caused by the chick attempting to digest inappropriate foods. They should be fed primarily soft food until they are six weeks old, when the standard seed mixture, with added red rape seed sprinkled on, should be provided.

The Second Round

Canary breeders must always guard against complacency. Whilst most fanciers are keen to make a successful start to each breeding season, it is when the chicks leave the nest and are weaned that attentions can wander. The second round seems a formality, but at this stage there are new chicks to cater for, as well as the original parent stock, and things can easily go wrong.

Caring for more birds means you are working harder in the breeding room. Simple matters such as feeding and watering, cleaning out, providing baths, and at the same time keeping an eye out for newly laid eggs or changed pairings, all impact on the breeding season. The answer is to keep on top of the routine jobs, particularly the cleaning routines with the onset of warmer weather, and generally all should be well.

Every fancier has difficult times, but there are always birds that simply do not achieve breeding condition, for a variety of reasons, and it is a mistake to devote too much time and energy on these unsuccessful birds, however good they may be. If they show little sign of wanting to breed, then simply turn them into flight cages and leave them to enjoy their exercise in preparation for an early moult. Another possibility is to turn two or three hens into a flight cage with a single cock bird, and equip the cage with several nest pans, just in case. These birds can be left to get on with things in their own good time, and if any chicks are produced, then they are a bonus. Either way, you have freed up valuable time to concentrate on those birds which are being successful for you, at a time when every second counts in your birdroom.

BASIC BREEDING PRINCIPLES

Certain basic breeding principles apply to the majority of canary breeds.

Pairings for Crested Breeds

The general practice when pairing to produce crested canaries such as Glosters, Stafford canaries, Crests and Lancashire canaries, is to pair a crested bird to a non-crested bird. The crest grows from a defect in the scull, which eventually forms the centre of the crest, and the crested factor is passed genetically into the offspring from either parent, and is not sex-linked. The theoretical expectation when mating a crested bird to a non-crested bird is 50 per cent crested chicks and 50 per cent non-crested chicks.

Whilst in theory the percentage of crested young can be increased slightly by pairing two crested birds together, in practice it is believed that a non-viability factor is potentially created, heightening the scull defect through the double factor pairing, and hence increasing the non-viability factor. From a heredity viewpoint, the non-crested parent cannot influence the production of crested offspring; instead the crested gene must always be inherited from the crested parent.

The crested gene is in fact dominant, and if possessed, the resultant chick must develop into a crested bird. The theoretical expectation from a crested parent is 50 per cent crested and 50 per cent non-crested young. Because of the dominance of the crest factor, these chicks will overcome the non-crest factor inherited from their second parent. The theoretical expectation in each nest is therefore that two out of every four chicks produced will be crested, and two will be non-crested birds.

These two 'crest-bred' chicks will not possess any inherent ability to pass on a crested gene, because they simply do not possess that gene in their biological make-up.

Matching Feather Types

All breeds of canary produce two distinctly different types of feathering, generally known as yellow and buff feathering. They are also known as gold or silver (Lizard canaries), or intensive and non-intensive (coloured canaries). During the nineteenth and at the turn of the twentieth centuries, the terms jonque and mealy were used when describing feather types, but these have fallen out of use. All the above terms relate to the structure of the feathers and not to their colour.

The feather type known as yellow enables coloured pigmentation to be seen which reaches the tip of the feather. The feather type known as buff only carries colouring to the edges of the feather, but not into the feather tips themselves, leaving a white border to each individual feather, which is devoid of colour. When overlaid, one on top of the other, these feathers show a less intense coloration, described perfectly as being mealy by nineteenth-century birdkeepers, but known collectively as buff feathering today.

It is widely agreed that the correct way to produce canaries displaying a wide variety of colours is by pairing buff-feathered canaries to yellow-feathered canaries. This general rule applies to all breeds of canary. Both cock and hen canaries can display yellow or buff feathering.

Achieving Specialized Colours

Cinnamon

The majority of canaries are available in a wide range of colours, all of which have been achieved by multiple generations of selective breeding, and all of which were derived originally from the same drab greyish-green wild canary. The majority of canaries are

Pairings using a Cinnamon cock bird

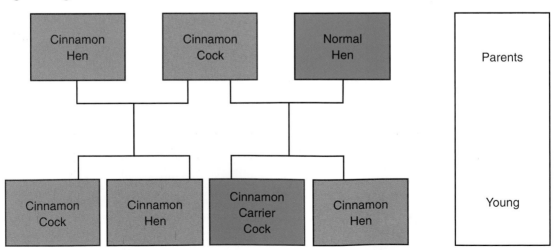

Pairings using a cinnamon cock bird – full cinnamon parents can only transmit the cinnamon gene to their offspring. The only influence on the cinnamon gene is by pairing to a normal parent, i.e. one that does not possess the cinnamon gene. In the subsequent generations, the cinnamon influence can be completely eradicated if required.

Pairings using a Cinnamon Carrier cock bird

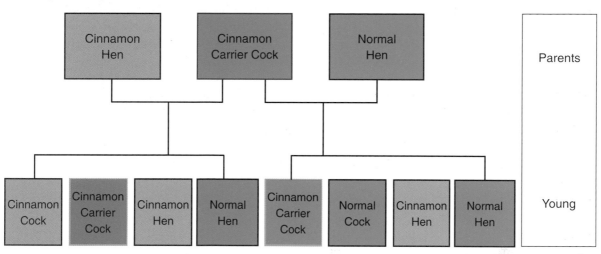

Pairings using a cinnamon carrier cock bird – whether the parents pass the cinammon gene or the normal gene on to their offspring will determine the sex and genetic make-up of their young.

Pairings using a Normal (devoid of cinnamon) cock bird

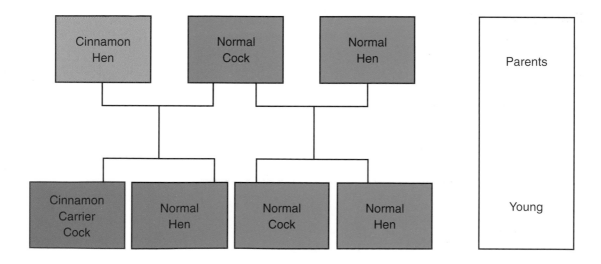

Pairings usIng a normal (i.e. devoid of cinnamon) cock bird – in this example, the only partner carrying the cinnamon gene is the hen. Because of the sex-linked nature of the cinnamon gene, the hen can only transmit the gene to her sons. These birds cannot develop any visual cinnamon colouring and will appear as normal birds visually – either clears, variegated green (or blue) or self-green (or blue). They will all carry the cinnamon gene in its hidden form, and will be able to transmit this gene to future generations.

now clear birds, devoid of markings, or they display small tick marks, through to those with larger patches of markings, known as variegated. These variegations are the effect of brown and black pigmentation, known as melanins, combining and overlaid on top of a yellow plumage ground colour. This combined effect displays as a greyish to green marking, depending upon the amount of melanin present. All these variations are perfectly normal, and part of every canary's genetic make-up.

When genes mutate, visual effects or changes occur. The most common of these is the cinnamon mutation. The cinnamon mutation simply denies the bird the ability to express any black melanins, leaving only the brown melanin present. Cinnamon canaries will therefore display brown variegation as opposed to green variegation, which would have been the case if the black melanins were present. They will also display deep plum-coloured eyes (known as red or pink eyes) instead of the usual black eyes, although this can be difficult to detect as the bird matures. A second phenomenon occurs around the cinnamon factor, in that it is known to be sex linked.

Both cock and hen canaries can be either full cinnamons, or what is termed as normal – that is, they can be completely devoid of the cinnamon gene. In addition, a cock bird can carry the cinnamon gene in hidden form, and is termed a cinnamon carrier cock bird. Carrier cocks cannot display their cinnamon factor through plumage, and in fact any variegation they display will be green or normal variegation. Hens do not have this ability to carry the cinnamon factor in hidden form at all.

Given that we know the inheritance of the cinnamon factor, it is possible to use this knowledge in our future pairings, to produce birds of the colour and sex that we require. The full range of possible pairings is as follows.

- Cinnamon cock x cinnamon hen: provides 100 per cent cinnamon young, both cocks and hens
- Carrier cock x cinnamon hen: produces cinnamon cocks and cinnamon carrier cocks, as well as cinnamon hens and normal hens
- Pairing the cinnamon cock with a normal hen: will result in cinnamon carrier cock birds and cinnamon hens, so this is a pairing to use to help automatically sex all young birds

PAIRINGS		**RESULTS**				
		Cinnamon cock	Carrier cock	Normal cock	Cinnamon hen	Normal hen
1	Normal cock x Normal Hen	no	no	yes	no	no
2	Normal cock x Cinnamon hen	no	yes	no	no	yes
3	Cinnamon cock x Normal hen	no	yes	no	yes	no
4	Cinnamon cock x Cinnamon hen	yes	no	no	yes	no
5	Carrier cock x Normal hen	no	yes	yes	yes	yes
6	Carrier cock x Cinnamon hen	yes	yes	no	yes	yes

Cinnamon inheritance table of expectations. This applies equally to both cinnamon and fawn canaries. As there are only six possible pairings for type canaries, every possible permutation is covered by this table.

Dominant White inheritance in canaries

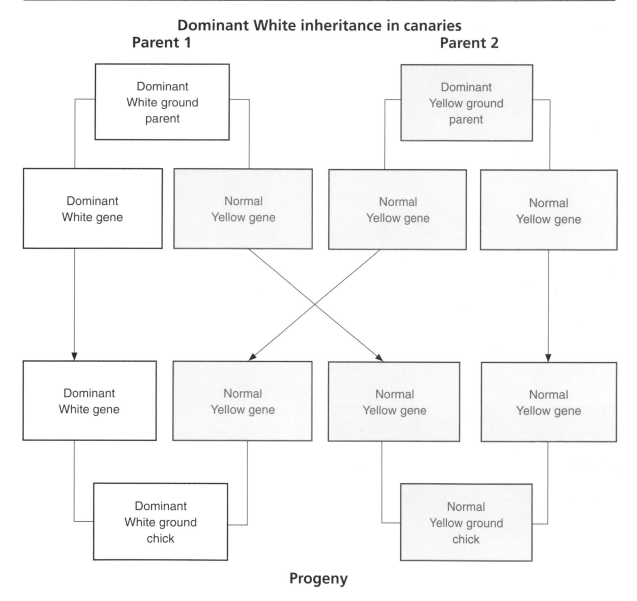

How the dominant white gene is inherited, mating a dominant white ground bird to a normal yellow ground bird.

- Pairing a carrier cock with a normal hen: produces a mixture of carrier cocks, normal cocks, cinnamon hens and normal hens
- Pairing a normal cock paired into a cinnamon hen: produces cinnamon carrier cocks and normal hens

Finally, as a rule of thumb, birds with an unknown background should be paired to variegated birds, because the plumage markings of any young birds produced will quickly help to determine the cinnamon factors of the parent stock, which could be masked if paired to clear birds, only to appear in future generations, to the confusion of the owner.

Dominant white inheritance showing non-viability factor

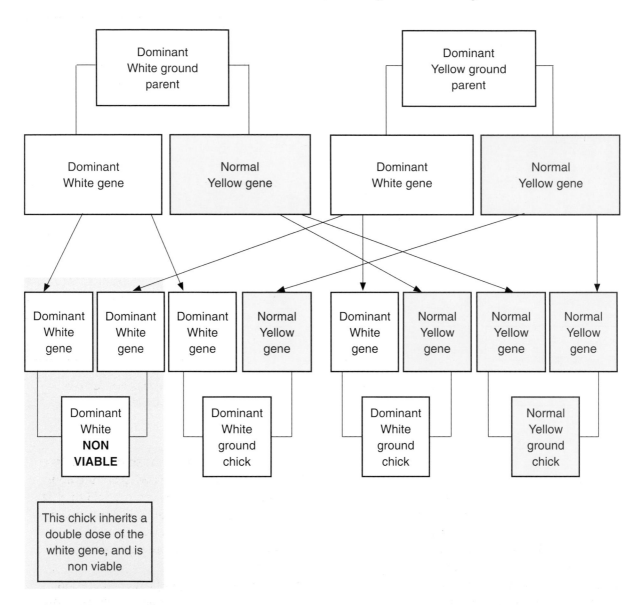

White or Allied Colours

White-ground canaries are becoming increasingly popular, particularly in continental Europe. White canaries are available in every breed of canary, and are of the forms known as either dominant white or recessive white. Although some experimental breeders are working with recessives, it is generally only the form known as dominant white which is found in type canary varieties.

White ground colour in dominant white canaries replaces the normal yellow ground colour, and means the bird cannot display any yellow or buff coloration in the body plumage, except for a very small amount in the wing and tail flights, and occasionally in the wing butts.

Variegation effects on plumage

	Yellow Ground Colour	White Ground Colour
Black and Brown Pigmentation	Visual Green Variegation	Visual Blue Variegation
Brown Pigmentation	Visual Cinnamon Variegation	Visual Fawn Variegation

Ground colour in canaries affects the end colours produced when the effects of melanin pigmentation are overlaid. These colour effects are entirely natural and are available in all varieties of type canary.

For the purposes of these notes, recessive is ignored.

As outlined earlier, the effect of melanins displayed in the bird's plumage produces visual variegation. The effect of black and brown melanins combined over a yellow ground colour produces a green-coloured variegation. This same pigmentation, when overlaid on to a 'white' ground bird, produces a slate grey colour, which the canary world terms as 'blue' variegation. Blue variegation is identical to green variegation, and is the 'normal' coloration of the canary when displayed on a white 'ground' colour, exactly as green variegation is the normal coloration when displayed on a 'yellow' ground coloured bird.

Similarly, it follows that any melanins displayed visually as 'brown' through the bird's feathering are known as cinnamon markings when overlaid on to a 'yellow' ground colour, and as fawn variegation when overlaid on to a 'white' ground coloured bird. The sex-linked inheritance characteristics which apply to cinnamons also apply to fawns, in exactly the same manner.

Type canaries displaying white feathering are known as dominant whites. They can only inherit the white gene from a white ground coloured parent bird, which may be either the male or the female bird.

Dominant whites must display their white 'ground colour' visually, and cannot carry the white gene in recessive (hidden) form. This means that a bird equipped with the dominant white gene must develop into a dominant white ground coloured bird. Given this, it follows that

Sex Determination in Canaries

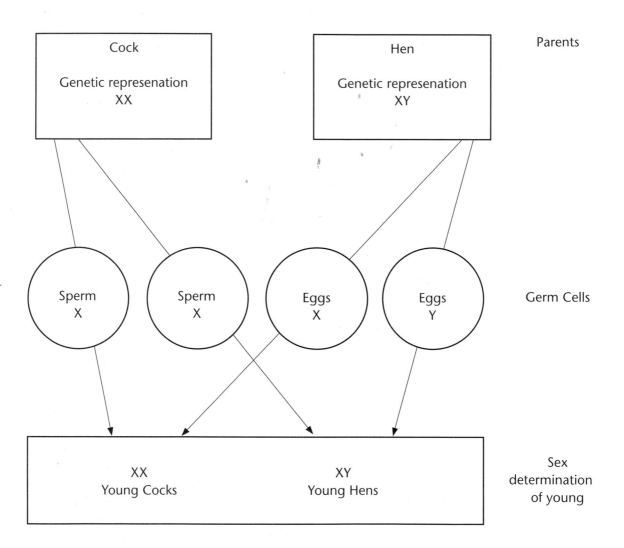

Sex determination in canaries – in terms of inheritance, the sex of a canary is always determined by the mother.

to breed a dominant white, one or other of the parents must be a white ground-coloured bird.

There is a school of thought that believes the dominant white gene to be lethal, if inherited from two parents simultaneously. Birds that possess the dominant white gene must develop into visual white canaries. The white factor is passed from the white parent in equal proportions to the normal gene, and must by nature dominate the normal gene inherited from the second yellow ground parent. This produces an average yield of 50 per cent white per nest. Pairing a dominant white to another dominant white would produce 50 per cent whites and 50 per cent normal (yellow ground) birds. Of the white birds, half would have received the white gene from only one of their parents, and would thrive, whilst half would have inherited the gene from both parents. This double factor is believed to be lethal (based on extensive trials conducted in Victorian times and not repeated in significant numbers since that time), and any resultant 'double factor' chick will die in the nest or not be reared to maturity.

The acceptable pairing therefore remains the white ground x the yellow ground bird.

Because of the nature of the dominant white gene, it is not possible to breed a dominant white from two yellow ground coloured parents, and even if any chicks are produced which are extremely pale in nest feather, they will ultimately moult out to become yellow ground coloured birds, because they do not possess the dominant white gene.

Finally, a word about feather quality amongst white ground canaries. Buff and yellow feathering exists in both white ground and yellow ground coloured birds.

Remember that the terms buff and yellow refer to the type of feather and not its colour. Whilst this is misleading to newcomers, in practice a longer, narrower feather will display more colour, and that colour will extend to the tip of the feather. This is a yellow feather type. A broader feather will not display the intense coloration, nor will it extend to the tip, and this is known as buff feather type.

Many bird keepers have continually paired white x buff for generation after generation, in the mistaken impression that by so doing they will reduce the slight amount of yellow coloration in the wing flights. In fact all that happens is that they will produce birds that lack type and quality. The only way to produce quality feathering is to continually match feather types yellow to buff, and this advice applies equally to both yellow and white ground coloured birds.

Experimental Breeding

Pioneering canary breeders set out to establish the breeds we know and recognize today, which are primarily known as type canaries. The work they undertook in itself took several generations to perfect, until true breeding canaries were produced which in turn would breed similar-looking birds.

Following the examples set by type canary breeders, coloured-canary breeders developed a breed of birds that were originally produced for their intense colour, using fertile hybrids from the Black-hooded Red Siskin, paired into canaries, with the ultimate aim of producing red and black canaries. A host of new colours was produced, and many more are still being produced, such as ivory, agate and dilute canaries, and new mutations including recessive factors and sexual dimorphic characteristics.

These new colours and characteristics are now well established, and more emphasis is being given to type within the colour section of our hobby.

More new breeds are emerging on a regular basis, introduced by dedicated fanciers breeding birds of different varieties, in order to achieve new aims. Recent examples are the Stafford canary and the Warwick canary, and no doubt more will in time be introduced, to take their place in our worldwide hobby. Today there are established procedures involved in gaining acceptance and ratification for any new breed, based on principles established by the COM (*Confederation Ornithologique Mondiale* – the World Ornithological Confederation), which is the accredited world body catering for canary breeds.

6 The Annual Moult

The key to the health and wellbeing of a canary is a successful annual moult. In the UK, canaries generally moult from July to September, with later bred birds completing their moult in October or November. Adults will moult as soon as they finish breeding, also completing in October or November.

As the canary breeding season comes to a close, the birds need to be prepared for a successful moult. For the fancier, the temptation to extend the breeding season, particularly if the numbers of chicks required have not been produced in the earlier months, is best avoided as the moult can be a trying time for birds, calling on all the reserves of energy the adults possess after the breeding season.

Young canaries produced during the first round start to moult when they are between ten and twelve weeks old, whilst later bred chicks often commence moulting at eight weeks of age. This is nature's way of ensuring they have the benefit of the warmer weather, abundant food resources and adequate foliage from which to hide from predators, whilst they go through the moulting process. In practical terms this means that canaries in the UK will moult from the end of June onwards, which is another reason why most fanciers aim to finish breeding during mid June.

By following a daily routine, moulting out canaries is easy, and the fancier can derive a great deal of satisfaction from the results, after completion of the moult.

PRACTICAL MOULTING CONSIDERATIONS

Controlling Light Levels

Light levels control the moult. Victorian breeders kept their moulting rooms darkened by whitewashing the windows or putting brown paper against the cage fronts to induce the birds to moult. Larger establishments went so far as to use special darkened moulting rooms consisting entirely of smaller cages; these also served to separate the stock from the breeding

This young Yorkshire canary is well advanced in its moult. The area around the head, face and neck are showing nest feathers and are lighter in colour, still to be moulted out, which will then be the same colour as the rest of the body. The tail will take approximately six weeks to grow.

room cages, which could then be cleaned and repaired, and confine the birds to smaller quarters, which helped to steady them for the show bench.

The overall effect of controlling the light levels in this way was to trick the birds' metabolism into thinking that the shortened daylight hours of winter had started, so they moulted quickly, simply to overcome the perils of the oncoming winter.

The same principles still hold true today. Now, breeders who use electric lighting simply switch it off after the breeding season to trigger the onset of the moult, while those who depend on natural lighting will reduce its effect with curtains, blinds or old-fashioned whitewash.

Victorian fanciers were of the opinion that the moult was to be treated almost as if it were an illness, but today we know differently. Except for the proviso that birds should remain undisturbed wherever possible, we know that the moult is not a time to be concerned about, as long as we follow a few simple steps and provide our canaries with a wholesome, nourishing diet in hygienic surroundings.

Housing for Moulting Stock

I allow my canaries to breed until they have reached the target quota (usually in June), which allows me to house my stock one bird to a cage throughout the birdroom. I let my adult cocks and adult hens moult out together in small groups in flight cages, which consist of breeding cages with the slides removed, turning them into flights from six to eighteen feet long. Nevertheless the same principles apply: effectively only one bird per cage, to avoid overcrowding.

Those fanciers possessing indoor aviaries may choose to use these in preference to flight cages when moulting out adult stock. I prefer to use flight cages, if cage room allows, because

these are less taxing on the moulting adult birds immediately following the demands of the breeding season. As these birds emerge from the moult, however, indoor aviaries are ideal for housing breeding stock that will not be required for the upcoming shows, as they will help to increase the stamina and condition of stock throughout the winter period, including the build-up to breeding.

Accommodating my adult stock in flights means that I can concentrate on training and moulting out my current year unflighted stock, knowing that the adult birds I wish to exhibit later in the year will soon become steady again, as they emerge from their moult.

PREPARING FOR THE FIRST MOULT

When weaning young stock, it is advisable to treat each individual with an insect preparation such as Ivermec to reduce any possibility of attack by mite. Nothing will reduce the condition of a young bird more quickly than mite, and fanciers need to be ever watchful. Birds can be weaned in small groups, then caged singly as they reach four or five weeks of age. By this time they will have enjoyed bathing together with their brothers and sisters, and this itself helps ensure their nest feathers remain in the best of condition, prior to the beginning of the moult.

Avoid Draughts

Draughts are the silent killer of numerous canaries, and there is no worse time to subject our birds to draughts than when they are in the middle of a heavy moult.

Birdrooms with safety porches rarely suffer draughts, although it is possible that open windows can be a problem, should the wind change direction. I have changed my current birdroom design to provide a baffle for when the wind whips round the corner during the winter months, and my canaries are far more content whichever cages they occupy.

The Advantages of Bathing

Canaries that learn to bath at an early age will continue to do so readily throughout their adult lives. Bathing is essential because it helps maintain feathering in top condition; it is also a wonderful aid to a successful moult because it helps open the feather follicles and release the nest feathers, which are replaced with adult plumage.

Herbal mite preparations are available that can be added to the bathing water, which will continue the fight against these unwanted pests and help the birds achieve a quick and successful moult.

THE PATTERN OF THE MOULT

Canaries moult their feathers in a set pattern, making it is easy to see when a bird is nearing the end of its moult. They first lose the feathering on matching sides of the body, in such a fashion as to maintain flight and guard against chills. New plumage will be noticed at first on the wing butts and down the sides of the breast. Next the back will be moulted, followed by the head. When a gap between head and body is clearly discernible, then superficially, only the head remains to be moulted.

The last visible feathers are those around the eyes – young birds look as if they are wearing spectacles at this time – and on top of the head. The head will appear spiky, with wax-like quills encasing the unexposed feathering. Spraying with tepid water helps to loosen these

casings, although in stubborn cases a quick comb through will help. There are still layers of feathers yet to develop, but these are simply padding, leading to an increase in apparent body size of the juvenile canary.

Neither the tail flights nor the wing flight feathers are moulted out during the initial moult, leading to the term 'unflighted' which is applied to canaries bred in the current year, until they have completed their second annual moult. This means that their nest feathering coloration is retained in their flight feathers, resulting in an attractive contrast between almost white wing and tail flights and a clear yellow or bright orange body colour, for example.

Feeding at this stage should revert to primarily a hard seed diet, and this hardening off process will see a marked improvement in the canary's overall condition.

COLOUR-FED BIRDS

Some breeds of canary are colour fed for exhibition purposes, whilst other breeds are not. Colour-fed varieties in type canaries include Norwich, Yorkshire and Lizard canaries.

Some breeders keep more than one variety of canary, and care must always be taken that the colour-fed birds are kept in separate cages, away from the non colour-fed varieties. Any elements of coloured soft food or water consumed will show through in the eventual plumage, and debar non-fed canaries from competition. To be safe, house the birds in a separate bank of cages and use different feeding pots, so that traces of colour food are not inadvertently transferred to these non-fed canaries.

It is also worth remembering that even canary varieties which are colour-fed will also include some plumage variants which are not required to be coloured. These are generally limited to white ground coloured canaries, or non colour-fed self green birds, allowing a natural grass-green colour to show in the final plumage.

A practical solution when using smaller birdrooms is to house non colour-fed birds in the topmost cages, with the colour-fed birds housed beneath them. This prevents foods dropping down from the upper cages into the lower cages and tainting the feed or water.

Modern Colour-Feeding Products and Methods

Modern colour feeding relies upon specially formulated, ready-mixed feeds based on a substance known as canthaxanthin. Products such as Carophyll are derived from this, and can be added to drinking water or to soft food supplies.

The advantage of preparing your own mixture is that you can regulate the intensity, and choose between adding colour to the water supply or mixing into the soft food on which your canaries have been weaned. My preference is to mix colour into the soft food, as this is more economical and causes far less staining in the birdroom.

To colour a bowl of soft food sufficient for forty or more canaries, sprinkle enough Carophyll to cover a small mustard spoon on to a grated hard-boiled egg. Stir this into your standard soft food mix and leave in the refrigerator overnight. The mix will turn a mid orange colour and be eaten with relish by your canaries the following morning. Used this way, Carophyll is extremely economic to use, and provides wonderfully balanced colour for even the most inexperienced fancier.

When to Colour Feed

Remembering that young canaries will moult from about ten weeks of age, you should start offering colour food to first round chicks in June, providing standard soft food for the remainder of your breeding stock.

Carophyll is added to basic soft food, or dissolved in water, to enhance the plumage colour of some canaries when they are moulting. The enriched colour will remain throughout the entire year, and revert to the natural colour again after the subsequent moult. Just a few grains of Carophyll orange as shown, when added to the base soft food, is sufficient to feed forty or more canaries.

The pale basic soft food and again, after a few grains of Carophyll have been added. The added food when offered throughout the moult will enhance the natural colour from a lemon shade to a salmon or rich orange shade, depending upon feather properties.

One proviso worthy of note concerns birds that have been plucked in the nest. These will commence growing new feathers immediately, so regardless of age, these young canaries should be offered colour food as soon as they commence weaning, even if it is still April by the calendar. This will help ensure they do not finish off patchy coloured because of their parents' misdemeanours. From the second round, the fledgling canaries will moult that little bit earlier, so the new chicks can be introduced to colour food at an early age; this means that by July, all your stock including the adults will be fed colour food in preparation for the moult.

New colour will emerge in the new feathers as they grow, showing firstly at the wing butts, then down the sides of the breast, before extending over the body and finally the head.

Throughout the year after the moult, keep a watchful eye for lost feathers which have already been replaced. It is quite common for canaries to lose an occasional feather here and there, which for colour fed varieties especially, can be disastrous for the shows. Provide colour food at least once a week throughout the year, until December when the shows are over, to guard against such feather losses.

MOULTING REQUIREMENTS FOR DIFFERENT VARIETIES

Different canary breeds have different moulting requirements. Gloster canaries with coronas will benefit from single cages (to prevent feather plucking), whilst consorts can be moulted in flights. Lizard canaries will benefit from single cages to avoid any discoloration to the neat rowings which plucking may cause. Equally, other varieties that are colour fed for exhibition such as Yorkshires and Norwich, also benefit from single cages, again to avoid feather plucking.

Smaller varieties such as Fifes can be moulted in small groups, but care should always be taken that the young birds do not nibble at other canaries' wings or tail feathers in search of something to play with.

SOFT MOULT

Soft moulting amongst canaries certainly appears to be on the increase, as anyone visiting any of our shows can confirm. (Soft moult is the term applied to an unseasonal, partial moult, which can quickly reduce the overall condition of the bird. A soft moult can be limited to a few body feathers, or can escalate to become almost an entire second moult, in severe cases.) Fanciers are experiencing difficulties where previously there were none. UK canaries that have been moulting between June and the end

STUCK IN THE MOULT

Occasionally a canary will appear to be stuck in the moult: it will appear listless, and although it may be seen to be constantly feeding, it will rapidly lose bodyweight. Conversely, sometimes a canary may not be able to start moulting, showing similar signs of distress. Any such birds should be given some saffron tea, an old-fashioned remedy but simple to administer and one that quite often works. Add a few strands of saffron to boiling water, then allow it to cool before offering to the birds. I generally make up some saffron tea and place it in the refrigerator for use the next day. Remove all drinking water from the cage for about an hour before you offer the saffron tea, and the birds will then drink their tea as soon as it is provided, which is the whole object of the exercise. Saffron is a natural product made from the crocus, and is available to purchase from most good supermarkets or health food stores. Why it works is one of the mysteries of the universe, but it definitely acts as a trigger to getting the bird back into condition. The tea shocks the system and is often all that is required to get things back on course. I usually also remove a bird into a different cage in the birdroom if it is having difficulties, as I believe that a change in local environment will also help it regain its natural condition.

An old fashioned remedy to help birds which are stuck in the moult. Brew the tea, refrigerate overnight, dilute as necessary and use in place of normal drinking water for a few days to help trigger the moult for any birds having difficulties in moulting.

of October would not generally provide any cause for alarm, as this is the normal moulting season.

I believe that our canaries no longer harden off as our birds did perhaps twenty or more years ago, and I wonder if the milder weather, especially through the winter months of October to December, is contributing to this in some way. I have lost count of the number of fanciers who tell me their birds would benefit from a few frosty mornings to tighten up their plumage.

Certainly we now offer soft food for longer than did previous generations of bird fanciers, and in my opinion, this contributes to the birds failing to harden off.

Artificial lighting and temperature changes may also be contributory factors, and I wonder whether we are thinking more of our own comfort in the birdroom than the comfort of our canaries.

Birds will drop a few feathers naturally throughout the course of a year, which should not be confused with a soft moult, and some canaries are simply unseasonal moulters. I have had a family of birds which moulted unseasonally in January, but were always ready to breed in May.

7 Training Canaries for Exhibition

Domesticated canaries are relatively timid birds, but they can be trained to trust their human keepers and to act in a much bolder manner. This takes time and patience, but training is an integral and extremely enjoyable and rewarding part of canary culture.

Imagine you are a judge of exhibition canaries and that you have to assess a class of young birds, all of almost identical age and maturity, and all, to the casual observer at least, identical to look at. But the birds as you approach them respond in panic, flying nervously in their cages, jumping from the cage floor to the cage roof or flying against the wires, and causing others to fly headlong around their cages. Some are visibly distressed and others have already damaged their plumage, and it is an impossible task to find a canary that conforms to the breed standard – or at least, a canary that will stay still long enough for you to assess against the breed standard!

This is why most fanciers accept that they have to train their exhibition canaries if they are to stand any chance of success on the show bench – besides which, unless your canaries are trained, how can you assess which birds to keep and which to dispose of, after a successful breeding season? And how are people who wish to purchase a canary going to choose one, if the birds won't stay still long enough to assess which are suitable?

Exhibition canaries are not pets. Pet canaries will grow to love and trust their owners, will approach them for titbits, may fly around the living room or sing to the radio or television, because over time they have been rewarded for their antics, and by repetition, have learned confidence in this behaviour. These antics are not required of an exhibition type or posture canary – although putting our birds through their paces from an early age is the surest route to success, since they must behave confidently in order to be competitive on the show bench.

Training is easily accomplished, with a little patience and knowledge. Different canary varieties have different needs: for example, Borders must travel across the two perches of their show cage, Yorkshire canaries must stand fearlessly to attention on the top perch, and canaries displayed in box cages need to be steady so the judge can assess them. But with a

Each bird occupies a single show cage, displayed for the public to view with ease. This picture was taken at the first every Yorkshire Canary exhibition in Athens, 2011. (Picture courtesy of Panos Paniagotides, Greece)

Winning birds line-up, Abano Terme, Italy.

little time and effort, each variety of canary can be trained to display to the best of its abilities. The following training guide will assist with all popular canary varieties, although training which is specific to particular breeds may also be advantageous, and may make that small difference from being placed second to winning the class.

BASIC TRAINING REQUIREMENTS

First of all, it is important to have the right equipment. Older show cages will serve admirably as training cages, whilst a simple training bench, so that you can view your birds at eye level, is a real asset in any birdroom. It allows you to work your canaries just as an experienced judge will do when judging at an exhibition, so they become accustomed to what is expected of them.

The Training Cage

Starting young is the key to successful show training. Over many generations the exhibition gene has been bred into our canaries, so all that is needed is to encourage our birds to display to advantage whilst they are in their show cages.

I start training my birds when they are about five weeks old. During weaning when the young birds are housed in small groups, I hang a training cage on to the stock cage, either removing the door or wiring it open to avoid it closing accidentally, thereby locking the young canaries in the training cage without adequate food supplies. The young birds quickly learn to hop in and out of the training cage, and the leaders will soon entice the more timid birds into the cage for an initial look around. A sprig of green food placed between the cage wires will encourage birds in.

There is no need to handle the training cage

This simple shelf acts as a show bench inside the birdroom. It can easily be removed when the stock cages are in use, and is placed at eye level, to allow easy assessment of the young birds.

at this stage – it is there for the young birds to familiarize themselves with it, so they become more confident in this new environment.

I know of at least one highly successful continental fancier who has adapted his training cages for feeding. The training cages hang permanently on each stock cage, and all food and water is supplied to the canaries in the training cage. There are several advantages to this approach. First, there is no food or water spillage in the stock cage, which will remain dry and can be kept clean simply by removing the paper sheet each day, which is more hygienic for the birds in general. More significantly, the canaries will become absolutely at home in their training cages, and all signs of nerves will disappear. They will also become familiar with the position of the feed and water stations, especially the water container,

which is particularly important because not drinking can often cause problems for young birds attending an exhibition for the first time. This system will not suit every fancier, simply because most will not have enough training cages, whilst many birdrooms are too narrow to permanently attach training cages and still leave the fancier room to go about their daily tasks unimpeded; however, this method certainly has its advantages.

After a few days in the weaning cages, I transfer my young canaries into single stock cages. As they enter the training cage, I slowly carry them to their new homes, where they hop in to inspect their fresh food and new surroundings.

Always speak calmly and gently to young canaries when handling them during the early stages of training, as this reassures them, and helps to prevent them leaping all over the cage in panic.

From this point forward, each time you enter the birdroom, hang the training cage on to each single cage, allowing the occupant to enter and leave at will, as you go about your tasks. It will only take a few minutes for each canary to investigate the training cage, and after they have done that, the cage can be repositioned on to another stock cage, and the process begun again.

The Training Bench

When the young birds show some confidence in the training cage, it is time to transfer the individual bird in its cage on to a training bench. It helps initially if the canary's cage is placed in between two empty training cages; by reducing the wide open space this gives it a feeling of added security.

Speak calmly to your birds to help overcome any nerves. After a couple of these outings small groups of birds can be placed side by side on the training bench, as they will no longer be flighty and will not scare each other. Placing an adult 'tutor' bird in the line-up helps at this stage, and the whole operation takes only a few minutes.

As you go about your tasks, calmly approach the training cage, letting each bird see your hands and gently moving them to encourage it to take up a show position, or to move across the perches. Finally, pick up the cage and hold it at eye level, as judges often do, before returning the birds to their stock cage.

Always avoid sudden movements. At this early stage more flighty canaries may hurl themselves against the cage wires and risk damaging their wings or tender young feet.

Training the Canary to Drink

It is important to provide drinking water during the latter stages of show cage training, especially if you use cage drinkers that are not of the traditional D-shape or open round design. Inadequate preparation on the part of the fancier in this respect may cause problems at a show, because if a canary won't drink at an exhibition it will very quickly start to look very dejected and to show obvious signs of distress, its eyes sunk in its head and its plumage fluffed. When faced with a bird in this condition judges will have little option but to mark the cage 'Soft', which effectively tells the visiting public and other fanciers that the canary is either not being looked after, or has not been adequately prepared.

By floating a few grains of condition seed or sprigs of green food on the water, inquisitive young birds will soon become accustomed to the position of the drinker, and will continue to find the water at shows, and so avoid such problems.

Exhibitions allow water pots to be placed inside the cage if these problems occur, and generally the bird will then find the water and have a drink; this will restore it to health

ABOVE: *Use slow hand movements to encourage the birds to feel comfortable in their training cage and display themselves to advantage.*

BELOW: *Only twenty-eight days old, but already this young bird is commencing show training.*

Floating seed or green food onto water drinkers is a great tip which encourages canaries to reach through and drink.

in a very short time, with no lasting damage done.

Establishing Training

Repetition is all that is required throughout the summer months. As the moult finishes, all that is needed to finish the birds' education is to take them for short trips inside their respective show cage carrying boxes, lifting them up, putting them down again, perhaps taking them on a few short car journeys, maybe to a local fancier's room where you might enjoy a mock show, comparing your birds as if you were the judges. All this will help your birds make the most of themselves when they are on the official show bench.

A specialist canary exhibition.

Some of the major prize winners at the Scottish National Exhibition in Edinburgh where the British Open Championship is held each year.

A FEW CAUTIONARY WORDS

During the early stages of the moult, young birds become too flighty to gain much benefit from training. No matter, they will remember their earlier training, and show themselves off to perfection as they emerge from the moult in their new plumage. Remember, untrained birds will let you down on the show bench, as judges cannot assess wild stock.

Do not renege on training the surplus birds that you do not initially plan to keep. They still need training, because if they are for sale, potential new owners must also be able to assess their qualities. Furthermore, despite the best care and attention, accidents will sometimes happen, which could mean that a reserve bird becomes a member of your exhibition team. The worst case scenario is that you lose a bird and need a permanent replacement from your available reserves – and if you have to select from untrained birds, you too could make the wrong choice.

The few minutes extra each day that you spend enjoying the company of your new crop of young birds and establishing their training is time well spent, adding to the overall enjoyment of your hobby.

One of the author's prize-winning birds.

8 Showing Canaries

Keeping canaries as a hobby involves no more than a bird in a cage inside the family home, or a back garden bird shed, or perhaps an aviary, where the wonderful sound of their singing is quite enough for many people. For others, though, it is only the beginning.

Exhibiting canaries takes our hobby to the next level, and whether you are considering exhibiting at local shows only, or wish to take your birds far and wide and compete with the best, you can be assured of one thing: your enjoyment from your birds will increase enormously as you meet other bird keepers, mix with other exhibitors, and share the highs and lows of competition.

EXHIBITING HISTORY AND STRUCTURE

Exhibiting canaries in the UK has a history going back well over 100 years. Not many shows then were reported, but there are documented reports of shows at the Crystal Palace in London dating back to approximately 1900, and of course regional shows were spoken of a long time before the turn of the nineteenth century.

Canary breeding then was still somewhat in its infancy, although several famous breeds had already established what were quickly to become national societies. Each of those societies had been formed with two distinct

These members of Liverpool Old Swan Cage Birds Society have just enjoyed a mixed variety canary table show at their regular monthly club meeting.

OPPOSITE: *A typical canary classification provided by the British Border Fancy Canary Club. Enter your birds in the correct classes, or they may not be judged!*

CLASSIFICATION
CHAMPION

Class no

1	Clear or Ticked Yellow Cock
2	Clear or Ticked Yellow Hen
3	Clear or Ticked Buff Cock
4	Clear or Ticked Buff Hen
5	Green Variegated Yellow Cock
6	Green Variegated Yellow Hen
7	Green Variegated Buff Cock
8	Green Variegated Buff Hen
9	Unflighted Clear Yellow Cock
10	Unflighted Clear Yellow Hen
11	Unflighted Clear Buff Cock
12	Unflighted Clear Buff Hen
13	Unflighted Ticked Yellow Cock
14	Unflighted Ticked Yellow Hen
15	Unflighted Ticked Buff Cock
16	Unflighted Ticked Buff Hen
17	Unflighted Green Variegated Yellow Cock
18	Unflighted Green Variegated Yellow Hen
19	Unflighted Green Variegated Buff Cock
20	Unflighted Green Variegated Buff Hen
21	Green Three Parts Dark Yellow Cock
22	Green Three Parts Dark Yellow Hen
23	Green Three Parts Dark Buff Cock
24	Green Three Parts Dark Buff Hen
25	Cinnamon Three Parts Dark Yellow Cock
26	Cinnamon Three Parts Dark Yellow Hen
27	Cinnamon Three Parts Dark Buff Cock
28	Cinnamon Three Parts Dark Buff Hen
29	Cinnamon Self or Foul Yellow Cock
30	Cinnamon Self or Foul Yellow Hen
31	Cinnamon Self or Foul Buff Cock
32	Cinnamon Self or Foul Buff Hen
33	Green, Self or Foul Yellow Cock
34	Green, Self or Foul Yellow Hen
35	Green, Self or Foul Buff Cock
36	Green, Self or Foul Buff Hen
37	Clear or Ticked White Cock
38	Clear or Ticked White Hen
39	Variegated White Cock (inc ¾ Dark)
40	Variegated White Hen (inc ¾ Dark)
41	Blue or Fawn Cock
42	Blue or Fawn Hen
43	Cinnamon Variegated Yellow Cock
44	Cinnamon Variegated Yellow Hen
45	Cinnamon Variegated Buff Cock
46	Cinnamon Variegated Buff Hen
47	Heavily Variegated Yellow or Buff Cock inc. Cinnamon
48	Heavily Variegated Yellow or Buff Hen inc. Cinnamon

objectives, which were broadly to promote the fancy of breeding and exhibiting specific canary breeds, and to extend the classification in all directions.

At a local level, canary breeders met every weekend and compared their birds. It was said that in the middle to late nineteenth century within the city of Bradford, West Yorkshire, it was possible to attend two different canary exhibitions every weekend of the year between October and the end of December, at different venues every time but never leaving the confines of Bradford. Canary exhibitions have been around for longer than any modern twenty-first-century bird keeper, and are still going strong today.

The objectives are to share and expand the canary hobby, to make lasting friendships with people who share a mutual interest, and simply, to compare your birds with those of your peers.

Exhibiting at Local Levels

Most areas of the UK are served by local mixed variety bird clubs. Though not as popular as in the past, these clubs serve a major function in that they introduce newer bird keepers to the fancy in general, and to exhibitions in particular. Most local clubs meet monthly, and have a mixed programme of events to keep their members entertained and to educate them in various aspects of the hobby. One such aspect is exhibiting.

Cage Bird Societies (CBS) will generally stage table shows at meetings throughout the year, and hold one or more annual exhibitions.

Club Table Shows

Club table shows are the most informal of the various exhibitions that canary breeders may attend, and are a perfect training ground for

younger canaries. Some shows are designated for young stock only, whilst others are open to birds of any age.

Classifications vary, but in general cater for, and are split into, different classes for adult and unflighted birds, cocks and hens. Generally speaking, the larger the show, the more varied the show classification. A more varied classification helps ensure that birds compete with others of their kind only, for example clear buff cock birds, or variegated yellow hen birds, of whatever variety.

Table shows still require birds to be staged in the standard exhibition cage for that particular breed, though it may need paper on the cage bottom to prevent seed or oat husks ending up on the meeting room floor. The birds will be caged for only a couple of hours, so as far as the young birds are concerned, the whole thing is like a trip out and they will benefit from their experience of mixing with other birds and bird fanciers in one room.

Another difference at table shows is that champion and novice exhibitors generally show together in the same class. This is a great opportunity for the novice, as it gives them the chance to directly compare their stock with the champion – and who knows, they may even win! As there are no patronage awards at stake, there is no loss of novice exhibition status involved, so the only person potentially to suffer is the champion who may get beaten by his protégés.

This all adds up to a bit of fun and some extra training for the birds taking part, prior to the start of the exhibition season proper in October or thereabouts.

Mixed Variety Club Shows

Mixed variety club shows are the 'bread and butter' events of the canary hobby, one of their objectives being to attract members of the public into the show hall to view the exhibits.

Many varieties will be unfamiliar to those who attend the show, but the whole spectacle may convert them into bird fanciers themselves.

In addition, these shows again act as a training ground for canaries that will eventually compete at the larger specialist shows throughout the UK, and many local champion exhibitors may be persuaded to attend if they are approached in the right manner.

Open Specialist Shows

These events sound grand, and generally attract many of the leading exhibitors from throughout the UK and Ireland. They are restricted to certain varieties of canary, for example Border canaries or Yorkshire canaries only.

Increasingly more specialist societies are joining forces with other societies and staging joint shows occupying just a single venue, generally as a means of sharing costs, but this approach also promotes a greater unity in the canary hobby, and is to be applauded. Nevertheless, each different segment of the show will usually be run autonomously, with its own judges, awards, different society patronages and so forth. Separate show secretaries and show schedules are the order of the day, and whilst some fanciers may stick rigidly to their own section, this is a great opportunity to view a variety of classes whilst in the joint show hall.

THE FIRST EXHIBITION

For the newcomer to the show scene there has to be a first time, and inevitably mistakes can occur. However, consider the process in a series of steps and this will increase the chances of getting things right: deciding which show to go to, which class to enter, how to prepare for the day itself, and what to do when you are there. These steps are outlined below.

Step One: Selecting a Show

As the year unfolds, lists of open shows are

A typical bird show.

printed in the canary fancy press. These are often grouped into separate lists for England, Ireland, Scotland and Wales, and listed in date order. Pin up the pages relevant to your circumstances in your birdroom, and you will be constantly reminded of the shows that you would like to go to: you can travel the country visiting places of interest, and enjoy a relaxed weekend away, simply by selecting a few shows out of your local area.

In addition to the open shows, there are many shows staged by CBS clubs (referred to above), classified as members events. These events also receive due publicity, and the best advice is to join your local society and become a part of your local 'birdkeeping community'.

For all but the smaller shows it is unlikely that you will be able to enter your birds on the day of the show. However, it takes only a little planning, and your weekly diary will soon be full!

Step Two: Apply for a Schedule

The next step is to apply for a schedule for your chosen event. Remember to include a stamped addressed envelope for its return – this will save the show secretary a few minutes at this critical time.

It is important to apply for your schedule two to three weeks before the show is due to take place, for two reasons: first, you need to select and prepare any birds you intend to exhibit; and second, your entries need to arrive on average one week before the show, so that cage labels and lifting cards can be returned in good time, whilst also allowing the promoting society to prepare a show catalogue.

Use a calendar: circle dates that meet your own programme and fit in with family plans, and then everyone involved will have the chance to look forward to a weekend away.

Step Three: Study the Schedule

Schedules provide two things: first, the classification; and second, the rules for the show. Take the classification first: if the show caters for mixed varieties of birds, then the classification will be wide and varied, and the schedule needs to be read thoroughly, to avoid mistakes. It will generally be split into four sections, catering for Canaries, Budgerigars, and British and Foreign birds. Each section will be further broken down into the different breeds or varieties, including the canary section.

Each section is also divided to classify the exhibitor – those with more experience are classed as champion exhibitors, and those newer to the hobby as novices. Moreover each canary variety has its own rules regarding the qualifications for an exhibitor's status, and these vary from breed to breed.

Classification for the Exhibitor

If an exhibitor is showing a particular variety for the first time but has previously kept and exhibited another variety – for example a Border canary breeder has taken up exhibiting Fife canaries – then that exhibitor will retain his previous status when exhibiting his new charges: once a champion, always a champion, is a rule that generally applies throughout the UK canary world. Conversely, if a breeder of a totally different species, for example budgerigars, takes up canaries, then his experiences with a non-canary variety do not apply, and that individual fancier has the choice of exhibiting as a novice or a champion.

Newcomers are best advised to join their local CBS club and gain some local experience before venturing on to the open show scene – although this is not always acceptable for the less patient fanciers! However, at your first open show you can exhibit in the novice section, where you will face competition from other, equally keen new fanciers, but without competing directly against 'expert' bird keepers. Note that it is the exhibitor, and not the actual bird, who is given status, so it is Mr X who is the champion, and not his birds. This means that should you, as a novice, purchase birds from Mr X, you can exhibit those birds in the novice section in your own name – and there is no shame in doing this, particularly in your early years in the hobby. We all have had to start somewhere, and until we have bred a few birds for ourselves, then we have no other choice than to exhibit newly purchased stock. Undoubtedly you will find more satisfaction from exhibiting birds you have bred yourself, but in your early days on the show scene simply taking part will almost certainly be its own reward.

The only general rule which is applied by most bird clubs is that a bird cannot be exhibited, in either champion or novice sections, under the person from whom it was purchased, until a minimum of thirty days has elapsed. Usually, 'breeders only' classes do not exist in the UK canary fancy, although this point is worth checking with your own specialist breed society, to be on the safe side.

Classification for the Canary

Classification governing birds will vary, but will differentiate between adult and unflighted birds, and cocks and hens, and will then classify the different colours, as yellow, buff, clear, variegated, cinnamon marked, and so on. Similar breakdowns apply to type canaries and colour canaries, old varieties, and so on, although they are called different names: for example, for 'yellow and buff' read 'intensive and non-intensive' in the Red canary section, or 'gold and silver' when exhibiting Lizards.

A major advantage at shows held by CBS clubs is that you can gain advice 'on the day' from other fanciers as to how to classify your

birds. In the world of open shows, however, entering 'in advance' means that you need to be more self-reliant.

It is often worth joining a specialist society for your chosen breed. Some societies provide a handbook which includes a detailed breakdown of the approved show classification, as well as the recognized show standard for your particular variety, and studying these will provide an insight into the correct way to classify your birds. Good specialist clubs will provide members with an annual handbook containing essential information about the breed, shows and other associated items, or will include this information on their website.

If you are still uncertain as to how to classify your birds, then speak to another local fancier. Again, CBS clubs are a great help in this respect, where a wealth of information is available for anyone willing to turn up to meetings and prepared to ask more experienced fanciers, who will be only too happy to give advice. Contact details can be found in the fancy press each week. Your original canary supplier is another valuable source of information, and will often be willing to help you at this time.

Step Four: Completing your Entry Form

It is a great help to the show secretary to enter your birds in numerical class order: you will save everyone time and avoid mistakes. Also if you are entering two or more birds in the same class, use a separate line on the entry form for each bird as the show secretary will note the cage number against each entry.

Most show entry forms are very similar, and contain space for your name and address, as well as class numbers and descriptions of the birds you are entering. A separate column usually exists for you to state which specialist clubs you have joined, and this information entitles you to compete for any special prizes these clubs have provided for competition.

Some clubs also run points competitions throughout the year, so it is advisable to indicate that you are eligible for these, particularly if you intend to compete at several events throughout the year.

There is also a column where you can nominate a price at which you would sell your bird; if this is not an option, then simply mark the column NFS ('not for sale').

Finally there is a section where the costs of the entry fees can be calculated, together with club membership, meals, catalogues and any donations you wish to make, so you can remit a cheque with your entries to save time on the day. (See the example entry form in Appendix 2, together with explanatory notes.)

Step Five: Keep a Copy of your Entries

Keep a copy of your entries, together with any special prize nominations you may have made, so that you can prepare the correct exhibits in advance. When your cage labels are returned, check these against your copy record: the class numbers should be the same as your original copy, and if a lifting card has been supplied, the class and cage numbers should be identical to the cage labels.

Mistakes, although rare, can happen, and it is too late if you discover on the actual day of the show that you have inadvertently brought the 'wrong bird'. If you notice an error, contact the show secretary immediately, and it will be rectified, even if it means obtaining a new cage label upon arrival at the show hall.

Step Six: Setting Out for the Show

Travelling to shows is routine for experienced fanciers, who know where they are going, and how long it will take to reach their destination. If you cannot travel with, or follow, an experienced fancier to your

chosen show, then pre-plan your journey. If you are late, the show manager can only hold up judging for so long before he marks your eventual arrival as 'too late', and withdraws your birds from the show.

Making a tick list is a good idea, and should include the following:

● Wash and prepare show cages
● Apply cage labels
● Include water drinkers
● Put the lifting card into the show case
● Note the show secretary's contact number, in case of emergencies
● Take your mobile phone
● Prepare a road map/satnav reference
● Check the journey distance and allow time for delays: arriving early is never a problem, arriving late is!

If you have to leave in the small hours of the morning, it makes sense to pack your birds the night before. They would be roosting anyway, so sleeping in the comfort of their show cage inside an open travelling case inside your birdroom is a great time saver, and helps overcome the age-old problem of placing a bird into the wrong cage, which can often happen in the early morning panic. You will enjoy the extra few minutes in bed before your alarm clock goes off, if nothing else!

Finally, enjoy the show, and offer to help out, if you plan to stay all day. There is always a need for extra stewards, and for help erecting and dismantling staging, watering birds, sweeping up, or helping with the raffle or on the door. All these activities help you enjoy your day, and ensure that you will be warmly welcomed back the following year – win, lose or draw!

Step Seven: The Close of the Show

Societies organize 'lifting time' differently, depending upon their particular needs. Some find that the most practical solution is queuing to await a section steward, then collecting one's birds, and having them checked out against the lifting card. Others simply ask exhibitors to gather their own birds and then wait for a steward to check and 'sign them out'; whilst still others work on the principle that everyone packs their birds and then waits patiently for the last man, when all are allowed home. Each system has its advantages and disadvantages, and all work reasonably well, but remember, patience is a virtue.

The best piece of advice given to me about the close of the show came from a veteran canary fancier. 'Don't be in a rush to lift your birds. They are easier to find when a few others have gone, and your nerves won't be affected by the wait. Pack them up, put them in the car, then help with the staging. For the sake of a few extra minutes, the roads won't be any busier, and you probably won't get home any earlier or any later, for that matter!'

Some shows allow exhibitors to watch the judging process, such as this exhibition in Izmir, Turkey, being judged by the author.

9 Breed Standards

The development of canaries has been a continuous process since the original wild canaries were imported into the United Kingdom many hundreds of years ago. Since that time, different breeds of canary have been developed using established selective breeding principles, with groups of dedicated breeders working steadfastly to achieve their chosen aim. Different canary categories were established, some catering solely for birds which became known as song canaries, and others that were bred especially for their shape and form. This group became known collectively as type or posture canaries, whilst a third group were bred expressly for their colour, with the intention of introducing new colour forms into the canary.

Today, by far the most popular breeds of canary are those known as type or posture canaries. Type canaries are bred throughout the world, in a great many different varieties. Procedures are now in place to help breeders establish, over a number of years, new type breeds, which in turn are both true breeding, and differ from other existing and already established varieties of canary. Ratification of any new breed is eventually granted by the COM (Confédération Ornithologique Mondial), the world ruling body for such matters, and includes such things as breed standards, and the aims and objectives of supporting organizations.

ESTABLISHED BREED STANDARDS

Some of the oldest established breeds of type canary have been developed in the United Kingdom. Our oldest breed, which still retains a large following, is the Lizard canary. Closely following the Lizard in terms of age are the Yorkshire canary, the Border canary and the Norwich canary, their names indicating their geographic places of origin. The most popular newer breeds of type canary are the Gloster canary, a small crested breed of canary, and the Fife canary, which originally was developed from the diminutive Border canary.

This chapter outlines the breed standards of the above-mentioned six most popular varieties of all established breeds of type canaries. From time to time these standards are updated, as determined by the leading specialist canary bodies and ratified by COM and the UK Canary Council. Standards are important as they help encourage every breeder to breed birds that conform to a given shape and quality, rather than simply breeding mongrel canaries.

All breeders of individual canary varieties are recommended to join their chosen breed specialist governing body, so they keep abreast of any changes within their own individual sector of the hobby.

THE BORDER FANCY CANARY

Border Fancy canaries get their name

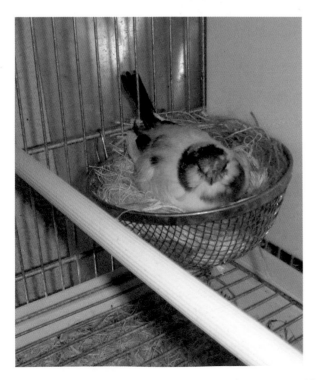

These four photographs all show the Border canary, which is popular worldwide. It was developed originally in Scotland, where its diminutive cousin, the Fife canary, was also developed. (Pictures courtesy of Panos Paniagotides, Greece)

Border Fancy Canary Standard of Excellence	**Points**
Head and neck Head well rounded and neat when viewed from an angle, beak fine, eyes clear an positioned to rest on an imaginary line drawn as an extension to the line between the upper and lower mandible of the beak, very slightly forward of a central point of the head. Neck in keeping with the head and flowing smoothly into the body lines and of sufficient length to give a free, jaunty look to the head carriage	10
Body Well filled and nicely rounded, running in a smooth downward curve from the gentle, smooth rise over the shoulders to the point of the tail, the line of the curve to the root of the tail always being downwards The chest also nicely rounded, but not heavy. Viewed from above and behind the body outline should be symmetrically pear shaped	15
Wings Compact and carried close to the body, covering the back, with primary and secondary flight feathers meeting at the tips. Outer flight tips meet at the root of the tail. Primaries and secondaries to be pointed	10
Legs and feet Of medium length and showing just a little thigh, the legs should be fine yet in harmony with the size of the bird allowing it to adopt a gay, jaunty stance. Feet in keeping with the legs, both to be clean and without blemish	5
Plumage Close, firm and fine in quality, presenting a smooth, silken glossy appearance, free from browness, frill and roughness	10
Tail Close packed and narrow, being nicely rounded and well filled in at the root	5
Position and carriage Semi-erect, standing at an angle of 60 degrees. Gay and jaunty with a full poise of the head	15
Colour Rich, soft and pure, as level in tint as possible throughout, but extreme depth and hardness, such as given by colour feeding, are 'debarred'. Any exhibit showing the effects of colour feeding will be disqualified	15
Size The length from the top of the head to the tip of the tail should not exceed 146mm (5¾in), length should be in proportion and balance with other features of the bird	5
Health Condition and cleanliness shall have due weight	10
TOTAL POINTS	**100**

from their place of origin, believed to be the Border counties linking England to Scotland. The Border was developed from the common canary, probably during the 1800s. It became popularly known as the 'Wee Gem' and was officially named the 'Border Fancy' canary in 1890. It did not take long for the Border canary of the day to become the most popular canary in Britain, and it was bred extensively in the UK before spreading throughout the world.

At the height of its popularity the Border had almost forty specialist societies in the UK catering for its development. A convention of clubs, known collectively as the Border Convention, was established to cater for the further development of the breed. In succeeding years there have been a number of significant changes to the ideal Border standard, which has been changed to keep pace with the development of the bird itself, led by groups of leading breeders and exhibitors.

No longer a small 'Wee Gem', the modern-day Border Fancy canary now rivals both the Norwich and Yorkshire canary in size.

Border Canary Standard of Excellence and Scale of Points

The first two essentials of a Border Fancy canary are *type* and *quality*. In general appearance it should be clean cut, lightly made, compact, proportional and close feathered, showing no tendency to heaviness, roughness or dullness, but giving the impression of fine quality and symmetry throughout. The table shows the scale of excellence that applies to the Border Fancy canary.

Further details regarding the Border canary are available from the British Border Fancy Canary Club (see Further Information at the back of this book).

THE FIFE FANCY CANARY

As the Border canary continued to evolve, some felt that it had outgrown its roots and had changed from the original small popular canary affordable for all. A move to revert back to the smaller, original Border canary gained momentum, and eventually a smaller bird was evolved from the original Border canary roots. As more fanciers took up this new breed of canary, regional clubs formed, until in 1984 the Fife Fancy Federation was formed. The 'object' of the Fife Fancy Federation is to coordinate, advance and encourage the culture, improvement and honourable exhibition of this special breed.

Since that milestone event, the Fife Fancy has gained popularity throughout the world, and continues to gain new admirers every year.

Fife Fancy Canary Standard of Excellence and Scale of Points

The Fife Fancy standard notes are as follows:

1. The grand essentials of a Fife Fancy are controlled roundness combined with type, quality and natural colour (that is, non colour-fed yellow, buff and white ground only) in a diminutive form. When all other points are equal, preference is to be given to the bird nearest to the ideal length.
2. Points are the maximum that can be awarded for a feature, but not the maximum it can be penalized for a serious fault: all features must be in balance.
3. It should be shown in the standard Border Fancy show cage with non-drinker perch moved in one wire – the drinker hole may be reduced in size for extra small birds.

Fife Fancy Canary Standard of Excellence		Points
Head	Small, round and neat when viewed from any angle. Dark, bright eyes near the centre. Beak fine	**10**
Body	Back well filled and nicely rounded but not heavy, the line gradually tapering to the vent	**10**
Wings	Compact, carried close to the body, meeting at the tips just below the root of the tail	**10**
Legs	Medium length showing little thigh. Feet proportionate	**5**
Plumage	Close, firm and fine, presenting a smooth, glossy, silky appearance and free from frill or roughness	**10**
Tail	Close packed and narrow, nicely rounded and filled in at the root	**5**
Position/ carriage	Semi-erect standing at about a 60-degree angle. Alert and jaunty, moving confidently between perches	**10**
Colour	Natural rich soft and pure, as level in tint as possible throughout	**10**
Condition	Clean and in perfect health	**5**
Size	Ideal length 108mm (4¼in) or less. Tending towards a diminutive bird	**25**
TOTAL POINTS		**100**

Further details regarding the Fife canary are available from the Fife Fancy Federation (*see* Further Information at the back of this book).

THE GLOSTER FANCY CANARY

The origins of the Gloster Fancy canary go back to the years after the end of World War I, in 1919 and 1920. Mrs Rogerson

OPPOSITE: *The diminutive Fife canary makes an ideal subject for a garden aviary. (Picture courtesy of Mary Holder, Scotland)*

from Gloucestershire was keenly interested in canaries, especially crested birds, but she strongly disliked the excessive amount of long, uncontrolled feather typical of the Crested canaries of the time. She believed that if she could breed a canary that was only half the size of the existing Crested canary and with a much smaller and neater crest, then such a canary would be far more attractive.

Mrs Rogerson therefore purchased some small crested Roller canaries and paired these to some small Border canaries. A second breeder, John McLay from Scotland, was also attempting to breed a miniature of the then quite popular Crested canary, and both were encouraged to exchange breeding

The Gloster canary is thickset yet diminutive. The crested Gloster is known as a Corona while the plain-headed bird is known as a Consort. (Picture courtesy of George Ioannides, Cyprus)

stock. In 1925 Mrs Rogerson entered two of her miniature crests at the London National Exhibition, and the Gloster canary was officially born. The crested Gloster was known as the Corona, whilst its breeding partner, which had a normal head, was known as the Consort.

THE LIZARD CANARY

The origins of the Lizard canary are unknown, but the variety is recognized as the oldest of all breeds of type or posture canaries, and is reputed to have played a part in the formation of several other breeds. Unlike other breeds of canary, the Lizard exists in only two forms, known as clear-capped and broken, or non-capped birds. They can be gold, silver or slate blue in colour. Variegated and clear birds are frowned upon, as they fail to display the plumage row markings of the Lizard, known as spangles, which are unique among canary breeds for their regularity and clarity. Lizards are at their best as unflighted birds, as their plumage row markings can show white tips after the completion of their first and subsequent adult moults.

Gloster Fancy Canary Standard of Excellence: Corona		Points
Head and neck	Neat, regular unbroken round shape, eye discernible	**15**
	With definite centre	**5**
Body	Back well filled and wings lying close thereto; full neck. Chest nicely rounded without prominence	**20**
Tail	Closely folded, well carried	**5**
Plumage	Close, firm, giving a clear appearance of good quality and natural colour	**15**
Carriage	Alert, quick, lively movement	**10**
Legs and feet	Medium length, no blemish	**5**
Size	Tendency to the diminutive	**15**
Condition	In good health and clean	**10**
	TOTAL POINTS	**100**

Gloster Fancy Canary Standard of Excellence: Consort		Points
Head and neck	Head broad, round at every point with good rise over the centre of the skull	**15**
Eyebrow	Heavy, showing brow	**5**
Body	Back well filled and wings laying close thereto; full neck, chest nicely rounded without prominence	**20**
Tail	Closely folded and well carried	**5**
Plumage	Close, firm, giving a clear-cut appearance of good quality, and good natural colour	**15**
Carriage	Alert, quick, lively movement	**10**
Legs and feet	Medium length, no blemish	**5**
Size	Tendency to the diminutive	**15**
Condition	In good health and clean	**10**
	TOTAL POINTS	**100**

Different types of Lizard canaries. Lizard canaries are bred with completely dark bodies and clear caps or with dark or partially dark head markings, known as 'broken caps'. They are available in Golden, Silver and Slate Blue colours.

The Lizard Canary Association of Great Britain Official Show Standard		Points
Spangles	For regularity and distinctness	25
Feather quality	For tightness and silkiness	15
Ground colour	For depth and evenness	10
Breast	For extent and regularity of row markings	10
Wings and tail	For neatness and darkness	10
Cap	For neatness and shape	10
Covert feathers	For lacings	5
Eyelash	For regularity and clarity	5
Beak, legs and feet	For darkness	5
Steadiness and staging		5
	TOTAL POINTS	**100**

Lizard Canary Standard of Excellence

A bird's condition is taken for granted. A bird which, in the opinion of the judge, is not in perfect health or which shows any physical defect, shall not be credited with any points for other virtues.

In classes of non-capped or nearly non-capped Lizards, points to a maximum of ten are awarded for the perfection of spangling on the head.

The wearing of rings is optional. If they are worn, closed or open rings may be used in accordance with the wishes of the exhibitor.

THE NORWICH PLAINHEAD CANARY

The Norwich canary owes its origin to the City of Norwich, and is believed to have been created by crossing the Lizard and, some believe, the London Fancy, with common canary stock. Norwich canaries were prized for their exquisite colour, created by judicious pairing, moulting and feeding. The secrets of how the colouring was obtained were closely guarded, and it was rumoured that a gentleman of standing in the local community stated that even the princely sum of £100 would not extract the secrets to which the Norwich owed its colouring – and £100 was quite a lot of money in the 1800s!

Further details may be obtained from the Norwich Canary Federation (*see* Further Information at the back of this book).

THE YORKSHIRE CANARY

The Yorkshire canary was originally bred by the woollen mill workers in and around the City of Bradford. The Yorkshire is the largest of the popular breeds of canary. It is bred to a particular standard or ideal model of

Norwich Plainhead Canary Standard of Excellence
Official Show Standard

		Points
Type	Short and cobby. Back broad and well filled in, showing a slight rise transversely. Chest broad and deep, giving an expansive curved front, and sweeping under therefrom in one full curve to the tail. Ideal length 152 to 159mm (6 to 6¼in). Stance or position at about an angle of 45 degrees	**25**
Head	Proportionately bold and assertive in its carriage. A full forehead rising from a short neat beak; well rounded over and across the skull. Cheeks full and clear featured, eye well placed and discernible	**10**
Neck	Short and thick, continuing the run from the back of the skull on to the shoulders, and from a full throat into the breast	**10**
Wings	Short and well braced, meeting nicely at the tips, to rest lightly yet closely on the rump	**10**
Tail	Short, closely packed, and well filled in at the root. Rigidly carried, giving an all-of-one-piece appearance with the body	**5**
Legs/feet	Legs well set back, feet perfect	**5**
Condition	In full bloom of perfect health. Bold, bouncing movement	**10**
Quality of feather	Close and fine in texture, presenting the smooth, silky plumage necessary to give a clean-cut contour	**10**
Colour	Rich, bright and level throughout, with sheen or brilliancy. Yellows a deep orange, buffs rich in ground and well mealed	**10**
Staging	Clean and correctly staged	**5**
	TOTAL POINTS	**100**

shape, size and position. It was said that the first Yorkshires were so long and slender that they could slip through a lady's wedding ring, indicating an elegant, slim breed of canary. Yorkshire canaries today are bred by dedicated breeders throughout the world to an exacting standard known as the Golding model.

Throughout its evolution the Yorkshire has maintained an upright, erect position similar to the hands of a clock when standing at 7.05 o'clock. The combination

The majestic Yorkshire is nicknamed the 'Gentleman of the fancy', due to its bold, fearless, erect stance.

of a bold, upright stance and deep shoulders tapering down to a slender waist has earned the Yorkshire the proud name of the 'Guardsman' of the fancy.

Further details may be obtained from the Yorkshire Canary Club (*see* Further Information at the back of this book).

The Yorkshire Canary Ideal Standard		Points
Head, neck and front	Head full round and clearly defined Back skull: deep carried back in line with rise of shoulders Eye: as near to the centre of the head as possible Shoulders: proportionately broad, rounded and carried well up to, and gradually merging into, the head Breast: full and deep, corresponding to the width and rise of the shoulders and carried up full to the base of the beak, which should be neat and fine	**20**
Body	Well rounded and gradually tapering throughout to the tail	**10**
Position	Attitude erect with fearless carriage, legs long without being stilty, and a slight lift of the tail	**25**
Feather	Close, short and tight. Wings proportionately long and evenly carried down the centre of the back and firmly set on a compact and closely folded tail	**25**
Size	Length approximately 171mm (6¾in) with corresponding symmetrical proportions	**10**
Condition	In good health and clean, of sound feather, colour pure and level	**10**
	TOTAL POINTS	**100**

The Large Crested canary is now on the endangered species list, as there are very few remaining pairs worldwide. (Pictures courtesy of Panos Paniagotides, Greece)

OTHER POPULAR TYPES

Other popular breeds of canary include the following.

- The Large Crested canary is now on the endangered species list, as there are very few remaining pairs left anywhere in the world.

- The Frilled canary is to many people an acquired taste. There are, however, many varieties of Frilled canaries, particularly in Europe.
- The Scots Fancy canary has a nervous action, which allows it to form a semi-circle as it displays in its show cage.

To many the Frilled canary is an acquired taste! There are many varieties, especially in Europe. (Pictures courtesy of Panos Paniagotides, Greece)

The Scots Fancy canary has a nervous action, allowing it to form a semi-circle as it displays in it's showcage. (Picture courtesy of Panos Paniagotides, Greece)

10   Healthcare

Domesticated canaries rely upon their owners exclusively for their health and wellbeing. As such it is our responsibility to care for them in the best way possible, and as responsible owners we must provide the following:

- An adequate environment, including housing, heating, lighting and cages or aviary space relevant to the number of birds kept at any one time
- A nutritious diet, meeting the needs of the birds at all times throughout the year
- An everyday working knowledge of the signs of good and bad health, and the means to treat common illnesses, conditions or ailments, without undue delay

The first two points have been dealt with thoroughly in Chapters 3 and 4. This chapter deals with general healthcare for canaries.

Whilst it is important to understand what constitutes a healthy canary, and to be equipped to treat common issues, there is no substitute for specialist advice, and whenever you are in any doubt concerning the health of your birds, I urge you to consult a fully qualified specialist avian veterinarian at the earliest opportunity.

It is curious to some that canaries which have failed to breed in certain birdrooms, will thrive and produce chicks in other establishments with little or no difficulty. The simple explanation is that the second fancier is more skilled at bird management, and caters for his birds' needs in a better way than the first fancier.

CANARIES

As a rule I have found that most canary keepers are attentive to their stock, and often instinctively know when their birds are not 100 per cent healthy. Keeping an eye out for the early signs of sickness or disease is the most useful role that any fancier can play in the healthcare of his stock. In the same way as for human ailments, early treatment is much better than late treatment, so always be alert for signs of trouble.

Canaries generally are active and bright eyed, and any that are not should be watched carefully. A bird sat hunched up with its eyes closed is displaying signs of stress – perhaps it has been in a draught, had a fright, or is suffering from mite or lice, or something more serious. Other signs to look out for include pumping its tail up and down, and watery droppings or signs of constipation; none of these will occur when a canary is in good health.

Common sense should prevail in the treatment of canaries. First, isolate any unhealthy bird and treat it immediately, using a hospital cage so you can control the temperature. A bird that is ill will often stop eating, living instead on its body fluids, and as these are depleted it will become dehydrated. Rehydrate the bird by using the specialist products readily available from those organizations offering bird-related products to the pet trade; these are often advertised in the fancy press, exhibition catalogues and on the internet.

A bird suffering shock is easily treated by isolating it and keeping it calm, and giving it a specially formulated stress treatment. As it perks up, it is easier to tell whether the problem is something serious or perhaps just a simple stomach disorder that has now passed.

If the bird does not recover quickly, immediately consider using the services of a qualified veterinarian. Several avian vets are listed by product manufacturers and receive publicity from time to time in the press, and again are often advertised through the world-wide web. Some organizations offer a remote diagnostic service over the telephone, or are willing to recommend you to a local practitioner.

Mite and lice will quickly break down the health of otherwise fit stock. The signs are as before, and any infestation can easily be discovered by holding the bird for a few moments, when any lice or mite present will be felt on your hands. Otherwise they can sometimes be seen, either as grey powdery dots or as fully grown mites, by blowing the feathers at the bird's rump, where they often congregate and lay their eggs. (Mite treatments are dealt with in detail, later in this chapter.)

The bird's droppings are a useful monitor: you will quickly become familiar with droppings from healthy stock, and anything out of the ordinary will also become immediately apparent. Wet or messy droppings, faeces of a different colour, and birds obviously struggling to pass droppings are major indicators that all is not well. A pumping tail, abnormal respiration and general listlessness are all indicators that point to health disorder, and which should be checked on a daily basis.

General health care such as clipping claws, trimming beaks, washing by hand or ensuring access to bath water should all become a regular part of your bird-keeping routine.

TREATING COMMON CONDITIONS AND ILLNESSES

Slipped Claw

Whilst not an illness, slipped claw is debilitating to a canary, but is usually curable if treated promptly. The condition generally affects younger birds between the ages of three and twelve weeks, simply because of the tender nature of their developing feet.

In birds with slipped claw, the rear toe slips under the ball of the foot, and points forward between the front three toes, so the claw is clearly visible. Effectively the canary can only grip the perch with its one good foot, resting the damaged foot on the surface of the perch.

The cause is generally that the bird has been startled, resulting in it flying on to the wires of its cage, or landing heavily on a perch at the far end of the cage.

Perches that are the wrong shape (perches should be oval shaped, and of varying thicknesses to allow exercise) or made from hardwood (perches should be made from softwood) are contributing factors, and slippery or smooth perching is also unsuitable for canaries.

If detected early, it is a simple matter to correct slipped claw: this is achieved by gently pulling the toe back, tying it to the bird's leg with a piece of wool or thinly cut masking tape, and keeping this on for a couple of weeks. The leg effectively acts as a splint, whilst the tape prevents the toe from returning to its earlier, unnatural position. A little 'play' should be left between the toe and the leg to which it is strapped, approximately 6mm (¼in), to ensure the toe and foot remain undamaged whilst the cure is effected.

My own current practice is to use strips of masking tape, cut approximately 3mm (⅛in) wide. These will eventually be nibbled off by the canary as it becomes cured, so there is no need to catch the bird to remove the dressing. If the

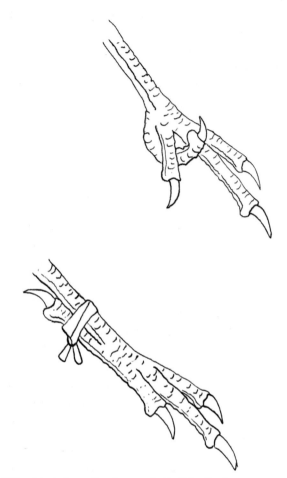

If the hind claw slips forward, tie it to the leg as a splint for a few days to effect a curve.

dressing is removed too early, however, the toe is likely to return to its damaged position; so always persevere, even if the canary removes the dressing every three or four days!

Stiff Claw

A more difficult problem to cure is stiff claw, where the rear toe becomes stiffened so that the bird cannot grip the perch; again this affects mainly young birds when their feet are tender. One solution that is usually successful is to remove the perching and replace it with thick string, forcing the birds to flex their toes to grip;

but again, the problem must be caught early for this to have any chance of success.

The best method I have found to correct stiff claw is to use a single string perch, with the string held taut by a weight suspended from the cage front. The string can be pinned to the back of the cage, at an approximate height of 10cm (4in). The canary will soon use the string to perch, and the balancing act it regularly performs will serve to exercise the foot and particularly the hind toe. The application of witch hazel or aloe vera sap as soon as the damage is discovered will help remove and soothe any bruising sustained. Applying a little Vaseline to the stiffened toe will help keep it supple, aiding recovery. Stiff claw can take three or four months to correct, depending upon the extent of damage sustained.

Of course, prevention is far better than cure, and providing the correct perching is a prerequisite in every birdroom. Young canaries in particular should be housed and weaned in small groups, without perches when they are first removed from their parents. After a few days, two or three low perches can be provided, approximately 7cm (3in) apart, to encourage them to hop from perch to perch, rather than flying from one end of the cage to the other and risking damage to their feet.

Claws in General

Canary nails grow continuously, and at certain times of the year when the bird is consuming more calcium in its diet, the growth can be quite rapid. As a general rule, nails should be only approximately 4mm (³/₁₆in) long, although this can vary from bird to bird. The structure of the nail is such that a central vein runs down the middle, almost to the end of the nail, and any growth after the end of this vein is 'dead'. As the nail grows, this 'dead' area extends, and can curl around making it difficult for the bird to perch, or to release itself from its perch.

Trimming nails can be accomplished easily with a pair of ordinary nail clippers. Hold the bird in one hand, and extend the toe towards a light source: looking towards the light, the central vein can be seen easily. Clip the nail slightly ahead of this vein, taking care not to cut into the vein. Generally speaking, it is only the front and rear nails which will need regular attention, perhaps every six weeks or so. If on occasion you accidentally nick the central vein, cauterize the wound with a lit match, which will immediately stem the bleeding and not cause the bird any undue harm.

Trimming Beaks

To a much lesser degree, canary beaks can also become overgrown. Ideally the upper and lower mandibles should come together, and should not be either undershot nor overshot. Mandibles that do not meet correctly can cause malnourishment in canaries, as they find it more difficult to shell seeds and to feed.

Again the cure is simply to trim the beak using nail clippers. Hold the canary in one hand, and place the thumb on the top of its head, which has the effect of keeping its mouth closed: like this the excess can be swiftly trimmed in a single snip, with no risk of damaging the bird's tongue.

Twisted mandibles should not be treated by the fancier, and veterinary advice should be sought.

Knocks and Sprains

Knocks and sprains can be treated with a weakened solution of witch hazel or aloe vera, or the various ointments that are generally kept in the domestic medicine chest.

Always make a point of checking if your canaries are perching correctly. Some will regularly perch on only one leg, with the second leg raised into their plumage, and this is quite normal behaviour and does not indicate any problem. It is wise however, to watch the birds as they move around looking for food, to check that they are using both legs and feet equally and with ease.

Scales on the Legs and Feet

Canaries' legs can display tell-tale signs of age. Healthy legs are pink and lustrous, or attractively dark in self-coloured birds, but as a bird ages, scales can appear on the legs and feet. This is generally nothing to worry about, although when the legs thicken considerably, this is often a sign that mites have burrowed under the skin and are causing discomfort to the bird. In this case there are a number of very effective mite preparations on the market, including Ivermectin, a product which will get rid of mite extremely effectively. Simply apply a single drop on to the bird's neck, and this will be absorbed through the skin and rid the birds from mite very quickly.

A little Vaseline applied to the legs each day will smother scaly leg mite and help soften the scales, which will ultimately reduce in severity. A number of proprietary lotions are also available to help treat scaly legs. Aloe vera sap applied directly on to the leg has a soothing effect, which also aids recovery.

Never attempt to remove leg scales by hand, as this can have a damaging effect on the bird. Frequent bathing and treatment as above will often prove effective.

Colds and Chills

Canaries are susceptible to draughts, which will quickly cause a decline in their general health. Always ensure that stock cages and aviaries are sheltered from prevailing winds, and whilst it is not always possible to cater for every eventuality, it is possible to anticipate problem areas and take appropriate measures, such as, for example, fitting fine netting across the inside wire door of the birdroom to act as a baffle against sudden winds.

Canaries can also catch a chill from bathing too late in the day, when their plumage has little chance of drying out before they roost.

Canaries suffering from draughts or chills will quickly lose condition, and look dejected and listless. They will be reluctant to move, and will sit hunched on their perch, often with their head tucked under their wings. Some will sneeze, and their droppings will become watery and will lose colour.

Affected birds need a tonic such as syrup of buckthorn, or simply a teaspoon of whisky, brandy or sherry in their drinking water, plus some well formulated conditioning seeds. In more extreme cases, the bird may have started to dehydrate, and this can only be corrected by supplying an electrolyte. Good results may be had in these cases by offering products which help replace the salts lost through the dehydration process.

A little extra heat from a hospital cage may or may not be necessary, but generally speaking, cures can usually be effected within twenty-four hours of noticing the problem.

Wheezing

There are three possible reasons for a canary to wheeze: it may be the symptom of a chill; in highly strung birds, wheezing can be a nervous reaction; or the wheeze may be caused by air sac mites.

It can be helpful to visit the birdroom in the evening, when the birds are roosting. Quietly approach the cage that houses your wheezing bird, and listen for the wheeze: if it is not evident, then it is a daytime problem and probably a sign of nerves, in which case a stress reliever given for a few days will often help.

Should the wheezing still be present, it may be that air sac mite is the problem. In mild cases, birds may be less vocal and will appear fluffed up, and are less active. In more advanced cases, symptoms such as sneezing, coughing, wheezing, squeaking, wet nostrils and open-mouth breathing are present, particularly after activities such as flying.

Air sac mite is a serious illness, which will result in death if left untreated. It can affect a whole group of canaries sharing the same air space, or in close contact with an infected bird. It is important to identify the root cause of the problem before treatment commences, in order to help ensure that it does not recur. Air sac mites can be treated, commonly by using Ivermectin, but the treatment protocol should be carefully supervised by a vet. Giving too little medication will be ineffective, and too much will lead to a massive die-off of these air-sac mites, which can then cause respiratory blockage.

Constipation

Canaries' droppings should be consistently firm, and passed with ease. Birds that have difficulties in passing motions may well be constipated. Tell-tale greenish stains on the plumage around the vent are also an indicator that all is not well. Canaries that are fed a mainly hard seed diet can sometimes become prone to constipation, characterized by the bird jerking down because it is straining to void, often raising its tail.

A small piece of bread dipped in milk and some fresh greens or fruit are usually enough to provide a quick, effective cure.

Diarrhoea

Diarrhoea or enteritis in canaries may be an indication of other problems that have upset the delicate stomach balance of the bird.

Calming the diarrhoea will help to indicate if another problem actually exists, or whether harmful gut flora had simply overpopulated the gut to the detriment of the bird.

Calming the gut can often be achieved by feeding strong cold tea administered through the drinking water or through a dropper, or by adding pure kaolin, available from most chemists. If these simple remedies do not work, an avian probiotic will help re-establish a good gut flora, which will swamp the existing harmful bacteria and thereby remove the problem.

FEATHER PROBLEMS

Canary plumage varies in quality from one bird to another, in a way similar to hair quality in human beings. The difference is that the canary's plumage is an insulator, and helps to regulate the bird's whole body temperature, so the good condition of that plumage is therefore of paramount importance, whatever its quality.

To maintain plumage in pristine condition, regular bathing is essential, as is a nutritious diet. Canaries that bathe early in the morning, two or three times per week will generally maintain perfect health, and their plumage will shine. Plumage that becomes dull and listless is an indicator that either the bird is not in perfect condition, or is not receiving all the necessary nutrients, minerals and proteins from its regular diet.

Soiled plumage, particularly around the vent area, is another indicator of trouble, and should always be investigated.

Feather 'Lumps'

As we have seen, canaries are paired by feather type, usually called 'yellow' or 'buff'. Whilst each category can be subdivided further, it is generally true that yellow feathers are longer, narrower and harder than their corresponding buff feathers, which are broader, of a more open weave, and consequently softer.

Canary feathers continue to grow for about three years, so as the birds mature, they become apparently larger, slightly longer, and have a fuller figure than in infancy. A potential disadvantage is that as the feathers grow, they lose some of their compactness, and become softer.

Annually during the moult, feathers are replaced by all canaries, growing through feather follicles in the skin. Each feather emerges in a waxy sheath, breaking through the surface and emerging as newly grown feathering. Birds with extremely soft feathering sometimes have difficulty in producing feathering capable of breaking through the skin surface, which means that the feather continues to grow beneath the surface of the skin, resulting in a lumpy growth under the skin; as it expands, adjacent feather follicles are damaged, and the problem increases. This condition is known throughout the fancy as 'feather lumps'.

The bird generally comes to no harm, and eventually the lump will break through the surface of the skin, and will ultimately drop off, although the canary will look unsightly until this occurs. Whilst surgery is possible to remove the lump, this course of action will damage further feather follicles, and the problem will undoubtedly recur as the next annual moult progresses.

Prevention is really the only cure to the problem of feather lumps, and this is achieved by correctly pairing canaries by matching the feather type, to ensure that a balanced, mid-sized feather is produced. Pairing two yellow-feathered birds for successive generations will result in under-feathered birds being produced, whilst in the same way continually pairing buff-feathered birds will ultimately produce large, ungainly offspring with extremely soft feathering and an increasing tendency to produce feather lumps.

Should you breed from a 'lumpy' canary?

That is for the individual breeder to decide, based on his knowledge of his birds and his ability to breed around the problem in future generations. The fact remains, however, that for two or three years in some cases, a canary may have been bred from with the potential to produce feather lumps, even though the problem has not emerged during those years.

THE PROBLEM OF MITE

Without doubt the scourge of all birds, and canaries in particular, has to be mite. Mite can appear from nowhere, and will quickly affect the overall health of any canary.

It is important to understand the life cycle and habits of this pest. Various types of mite exist, some which live on the bird, and others which live in cracks and crevices in the cages, feeding off the bird at night time. Protecting against mite is therefore a dual process. The most damaging mite to canaries is red mite.

Red Mite

The red mite is a small ectoparasite which feeds on the blood, feathers, skin or scales of birds. The mites can be seen by the naked eye; heavy infestations can seriously damage health, and in extreme cases can cause death. Red mite are active mainly during the night time, feeding on the birds for typically one to two hours, before returning to hiding places in cracks and crevices, seedbins and such like, where they mate and lay eggs. Red mite eggs are small (0.4 x 0.25mm), oval and opalescent white; they hatch in two to three days into six-legged larvae, which moult within twenty-four hours of hatching into an eight-legged protonymph, and subsequently to a deutonymph, and then into an adult form. Under favourable warm conditions a mite can complete a life cycle from egg to egg within seven days. In ideal conditions the female red mite can lay 120,000 eggs, which will clearly result in a serious infestation if left untreated.

Mites cause significant stress to birds, resulting in a reduction in breeding condition, and ultimately in anaemia and death, particularly when they infest the nests of chicks during the breeding season. Mites have been implicated as carriers of significant avian diseases including chicken pox virus, Newcastle virus and fowl typhoid.

Red mite can survive for up to eight months without feeding, and their appearance varies: they may be red, black or grey, relative to when they last fed. After mites have fed, they appear as red dots that turn to red blood when squashed, but because they feed at night, they are difficult to spot during the daytime unless you know what to look out for. Typically, look for white/grey dust around cracks in the corners or joints of the cage, around perch ends and under cage trays. Birds will be restless at night, and during the daytime will display signs of severe skin irritation from the biting mites.

It usually takes several attempts to get rid of red mite, so perseverance and vigilance are called for. Thankfully there are several proprietary products and treatments available that will eradicate mite, ranging from aerosol sprays to insect powders, to bathing treatments and naturally produced treatments.

Mite Treatments

Eliminating mites is a two-stage process which involves treating first the birdroom, cages and equipment, and second, the bird itself. There are also two simple points to remember: first, in order to stand any chance of success, the mite seven-day life cycle must be broken. Second, it is crucial to appreciate that the war against mite is an ongoing battle, and treatments must be repeated at regular intervals, rather than waiting and reacting to attacks after they have occurred.

Old-fashioned Cures

Old-time birdkeepers treated mite by applying creosote to birdroom walls and cage joints, dipping perch ends into paraffin, or painting paraffin or coca cola around cage cracks and corners. This reduced the waxy coating of any mite, which died by dehydration as a result. Vaseline applied to cracks and crevices in the birdroom also helped, and carbolic soap was another effective natural barrier against mite.

Insecticides

Numerous products exist, which generally operate as contact insecticides, killing mite on contact. These are available in powder, spray and liquid forms.

Powders are used to dust birds, perches, cage trays and nest linings; they are effective for several weeks, but need reapplying when the cages and so on are cleaned. Sprays are only effective when in direct contact with various mites and lice, which may hide under the feathers, if still on the bird. Ardap is a particularly effective spray, and has become increasingly popular amongst birdkeepers during the twenty-first century.

Liquids can generally be diluted and used to wash cages and so on, on a regular basis, paying particular attention to cage joints and cracks and other likely hiding places. Duramitex was a popular concentrated liquid solution that was diluted with water and then sprayed into cracks and crevices from a plant sprayer. However, it was based on the active ingredient malathion, an organophosphate that is now banned, so has now been replaced by Duramitex Plus, which remains pesticide free.

There are several other, non-toxic liquid products which act by reducing the wax coating and dehydrating the mite, or which contain repellents that mites do not like. This new range of products is effective on both mites and eggs, and is perfectly safe to use on canaries and other birds.

Ivermectin

Now available without prescription, Ivermectin is a liquid applied directly on to the skin using a dropper or cotton bud; it is extremely effective at eliminating adult mites that bite and feed off canaries, but it will not kill mites at earlier stages of development. Because of this, it should be considered as only a partial cure, and should be used in conjunction with other measures.

Natural Mite Remedies

Various natural insecticides and deterrents can help against red mite infestation, including some products readily available for human use: these include tea tree, citronella, peppermint, eucalyptus, lemongrass, cedarwood oils, soya bean oil, diatoms and garlic. By far the most effective are diatomaceous earth and garlic.

Diatomaceous earth (also known commercially as DE powder) consists of the microskeletons of fossilized remains of deceased diatoms, a type of algae found in both sea water and fresh water. It is very safe to use and can be dusted around the cage floor and on the ends of perches, and used as a powder on the bird itself. Diatom has microscopically sharp edges and works by piercing the outer waxy coating of the mite, which will dry up and die, usually within a matter of hours. There is no chemical toxicity since diatom controls insects by physical means rather than chemical.

In addition, diatoms can be added to the feed of canaries and other animals, and when consumed will act as a de-wormer, ridding the canary of internal parasites as well as external mite.

Garlic has numerous health benefits as well as being a natural insecticide. It is believed that red mites don't like the smell that comes off the skin or the taste of the blood after garlic has been eaten. A fresh garlic clove can be placed in the drinking water, or fed directly to birds. Garlic cloves can also be blended into the soft food, and are eaten readily by canaries.

Treating Cages and Equipment

Thoroughly clean, wash and disinfect all cages using any of the household products readily available. There are also a number of cleaning products specifically designed for use with birds; these are advertised regularly in the national birdkeeping press and on avian stockist websites, and in addition to the cleansing properties of general detergents, they are also effective against various yeasts, viruses and fungi. This means that your cleansing operations are not only destroying mite, but also many latent germs and bacteria.

Furthermore, after washing and preparing your cages, consider it a good opportunity to apply a fresh coat of paint. It is perfectly possible to mix a long-lasting mite treatment into the paint, such as Duramitex Plus or similar, for added security against future infestation. When the cages are dry, the application of an anti-mite aerosol into each cage prepares it for habitation. An alternative to an aerosol is to puff some diatomaceous earth powder around the cage, which will provide a further barrier against mite infestation.

Cages should be kept pest-free by the continued use of disinfectants, by spraying with mite preparations, and powdering each time the cages are cleaned. Moreover, never neglect the underside of cage trays and so on, as these are often favourite hiding places for mite.

A simple point to remember, although sadly often forgotten, is never to return a bird into a clean cage until it has been protected itself against mite. There is little point in cleaning cages if they are reinfested by their first new occupant.

Treating the Birds

Canaries need to be treated for mite in two stages to ensure that not only are the mite eliminated, but also their eggs. As we have seen, the life cycle of mite from egg to hatching is between five and seven days, with maturity and the ability to produce more eggs a further seven days. This means that you need to break the life cycle to eradicate mite from your birdroom.

A wide range of products exists, in aerosol, liquid or powder forms. Some are designed as pesticides, whilst other advanced products inhibit the reproductive cycle: the choice is yours. Aerosols can be a hit or miss affair if the canaries are flying around, and a more effective method is to hold the bird in your hand with the tail held down. Position the aerosol spray about 45cm (18in) away, and spray the rump area of the bird. Alternatively, spray a little of the contents into an egg cup, then dab a cotton bud into the solution, and apply directly to the skin of the bird, to be absorbed into the bloodstream.

When using a liquid mite preparation such as Ivermectin, again hold the bird, gently flipping the neck to one side. From above, the back of the neck is revealed, and using an eye dropper, a single drop of liquid mite preparation can be applied directly on to the skin. This will be absorbed into the bloodstream and will quickly destroy any mite that are feeding from the bird. Applying the preparation to the neck means that the canary cannot nibble at the site, so absorption into the bloodstream is guaranteed.

Applying mite powder is simple. Lay out a sheet of newspaper, and hold the bird over this. Take a pinch of powder and apply it to the rump area and also to the neck, working it into the feathering as you go. Hold the bird for a few seconds before releasing it back into a clean cage. Any spilled powder can be used on your next patient, so no waste! The key with any mite preparation is to treat the birds twice, at an interval of no more than one week. This is because any eggs laid are unaffected by the first application, and so need treating within a day or so of hatching, before the juvenile mite are mature enough to commence egg laying themselves. Simply repeat the processes outlined above, seven days after the first treatment.

My own preferences are for an initial liquid mite treatment (two applications at a weekly interval), followed by a double powder treatment four weeks later, with a final powder treatment when the birds are placed into their respective breeding cages. That should see a

relatively trouble-free first round, if a few simple extra precautions are taken along the way.

How exactly mite arrives in our birdrooms will for ever be a mystery, though no doubt they are airborne, or hitch a ride back after our birds have been to shows, and of course are also present in the seeds we buy. There can be little doubt of this, since many of us now follow a regime whereby all our show cages and birds are sprayed against mite before they are returned to our birdrooms.

Sadly, mite appears to be an ever-present part of livestock husbandry, and so the best approach we can adopt is one of constant vigilance. I also believe that it matters little what preparations you buy, as long as you change them every few years, so that the mite cannot build up a resistance.

Appendix 1: Canary Management

HOUSING

- Always ensure your birds are kept in draught-proof accommodation. Draughts can easily kill or reduce the health of canaries.
- Regularly clean the stock cages. Clean cages mean the birds do not soil themselves so easily, and with improved plumage they will be better insulated to cope with damp weather.
- Paint stock cages annually if using emulsion paint, or biannually with gloss. Freshly painted cages rarely harbour mite. Those who do not like painted cages could use varnish instead.
- Repainting is never a substitute for guarding against mite – mix some Duramitex Plus or similar into the paint, and always spray and treat cages, even if newly painted.
- Never keep more stock than can be comfortably maintained. Time spent on feeding, cleaning and the myriad other tasks all eat into your own free time. Your hobby should be just that, and not an all-consuming passion.
- Overcrowding is a sure way of creating stressful conditions. If you have too many birds, dispose of some either through the trade to other breeders, or to local nursing homes or schools.
- Use a predefined schedule for heating and lighting. Random heat and light causes birds to moult. If heat is used it should be introduced gradually, and when using lights, work to a timer system, with a dimmer system when the lights go out.
- Have a place for everything, and keep everything in its place. This maxim really works in the birdroom.

FEEDING

- Establish a workable routine that fits into your own living and working patterns and which you can maintain.
- Feed according to the seasons of the year. Emulate nature to achieve the best results and adapt your feeds to match the seasons of the year, and how the wild birds feed.
- Be systematic in your approach. Haphazard feeding, cleaning and management lead to poor results and a poor quality of life for your canaries.
- Do not over-buy seeds or soft food. Work on a six- to eight-week seed cycle and enough soft food to feed your birds throughout the breeding and moulting seasons.

BREEDING

- Breed only as many birds as you can comfortably house. One bird to a cage is a golden rule!
- Prepare your stock in advance. Birds breed when in perfect breeding condition, which can only be achieved by preparation.

- Purchase soft feeds to last the entire season: soft food is essential, so obtain sufficient to last the breeding season, so you do not run out.
- Plan your pairings to suit your needs. Matched pairs are often the best way for newcomers to proceed. If necessary, ask a local experienced fancier to match your birds.
- Pair best to best if they are compatible. Work around your more successful birds both on the show bench and in the breeding room.

EXHIBITING

- Support local mixed shows as well as specialist shows. Local clubs are the lifeline of the canary hobby, so never neglect your obligation to support your local clubs.

- Enter in advance and include an SAE for the return of labels, lifting cards and so on. Planning for shows is just as important as planning for the breeding season.
- Keep a copy of your entries, then you will be sure which birds to prepare and take to the shows.
- Never exhibit an unhealthy bird. Unfit birds will never win and could die if subjected to the stress of a show.
- Ensure your show cages are clean. Well run shows will refuse entry to birds in dirty cages, and you have a duty of care to maintain your birds and their cages in good condition.
- Take both wins and defeats in your stride: nobody likes a poor loser, and the same goes for a gloating winner.

Appendix 2: Sample Entry Form

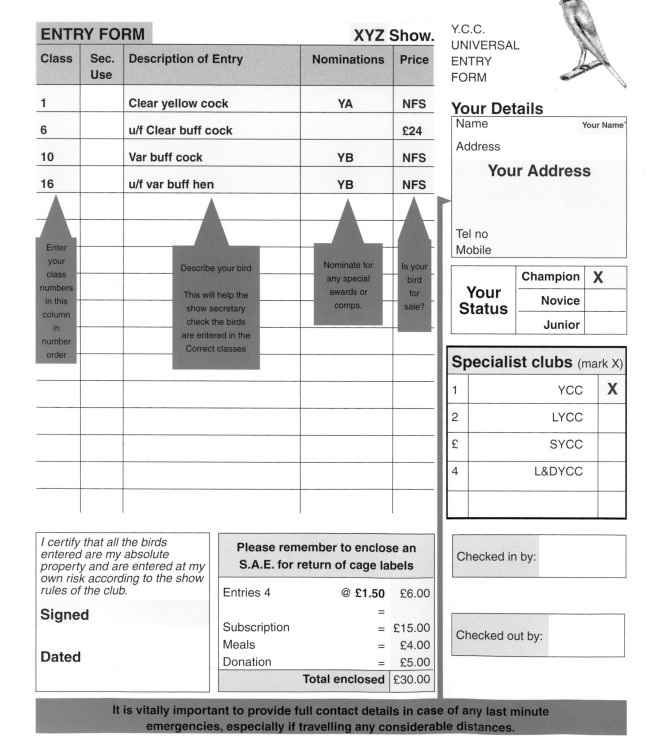

ENTRY FORM **XYZ Show.**

Y.C.C.
UNIVERSAL
ENTRY
FORM

Class	Sec. Use	Description of Entry	Nominations	Price
1		Clear yellow cock	YA	NFS
6		u/f Clear buff cock		£24
10		Var buff cock	YB	NFS
16		u/f var buff hen	YB	NFS

Enter your class numbers in this column in number order

Describe your bird

This will help the show secretary check the birds are entered in the Correct classes

Nominate for any special awards or comps.

Is your bird for sale?

Your Details

Name — Your Name

Address

Your Address

Tel no
Mobile

Your Status	Champion	X
	Novice	
	Junior	

Specialist clubs (mark X)

1	YCC	X
2	LYCC	
£	SYCC	
4	L&DYCC	

I certify that all the birds entered are my absolute property and are entered at my own risk according to the show rules of the club.

Signed

Dated

Please remember to enclose an S.A.E. for return of cage labels

Entries 4	@ **£1.50**	£6.00
	=	
Subscription	=	£15.00
Meals	=	£4.00
Donation	=	£5.00
Total enclosed		£30.00

Checked in by:

Checked out by:

It is vitally important to provide full contact details in case of any last minute emergencies, especially if travelling any considerable distances.

Glossary

adult Bird which has undergone its first full moult, moulting out its wing flight and tail flight feathers. The bird is a minimum of one year old at this stage. *See also* **flighted** and **over-year**.

allele (allelomorph) One of a pair of alternative heritable characters. When the male's two X chromosomes are the same, they will develop into true green or cinnamon birds. These are known as the normal alleles (true green) or mutant alleles (true cinnamon). When one X chromosome is different from the other, this will result in visual green birds (the dominant colour) each carrying the cinnamon (mutated) gene in 'recessive' or hidden form. Because hens have only one X chromosome which is always inherited from their father and which must be either the true breeding green or the true breeding cinnamon characteristic, then a hen must be either a cinnamon or a 'normal' – she cannot physically be a cinnamon carrier. *See also* **chromosome**.

blue A white ground bird with both black and brown melanins present, which together combine to form 'blue' variegation. *See also* **green** and **normal**.

breeding A loose term applied when attempting to raise young birds to adulthood. There are several types of breeding system: pair breeding, running one cock with several hens, and colony breeding. Most advanced fanciers practise line breeding, using also out-cross and inbreeding as necessary, in the creation of their stud.

buff A particular feather type. Buff feathers are broad and open, and the colouring does not extend to the feather tip, resulting in a frosted appearance, often called 'frosting' or 'mealing'. Buff birds are a pale lemon colour when not colour fed, deepening in shades up to a rich salmon colour, when colour fed. *See also* **frosted** and **mealy** and **silver**.

Carophyll Otherwise known as canthaxanthin. A product extracted from mushrooms used to enhance the natural colour of several varieties of exhibition canary. Manufactured by Roche Products, and a registered trade mark. Sold in three forms: Carophyll yellow, orange and red. Carophyll yellow is not often used by canary breeders, but both orange and red are widely used. *See also* **orange (Carophyll)** and **red (Carophyll)**.

cell Nucleus and protoplasm composing the body of a bird.

chromosome Bodies present in the cell which carry the genes. In terms of sex chromosomes, cock birds inherit the X chromosome from both parents, thereby having two X chromosomes, whilst hens inherit X from their fathers and the Y chromosome from their mothers in every case. *See also* **X chromosome** and **Y chromosome**.

cinnamon   Canaries are capable of expressing two colour pigments or melanins, black and brown, which together combine to form 'green' variegation. When the black pigmentation cannot be expressed in either the bird's plumage or eye colour, the bird is known as cinnamon, displaying brown feathering and red eye colour, with all traces of black removed. The cinnamon gene displayed on a white ground coloured bird is termed fawn. Cinnamon is a sex-linked, recessive factor. Pairings to breed cinnamons are as follows:

● Normal cock × normal hen:
  Results = normal cocks, normal hens
● Normal cock × cinnamon hen
  Results = cinnamon carrier cocks, normal hens
● Cinnamon cock × normal hen
  Results = cinnamon carrier cocks, normal cocks, cinnamon hens
● Carrier cock × normal hen
  Results = cinnamon carrier cocks, normal cocks, cinnamon hens, normal hens
● Carrier cock × cinnamon hen
  Results = cinnamon cocks, cinnamon carrier cocks, cinnamon hens, normal hens
● Cinnamon cock × cinnamon hen
  Results = cinnamon cocks, cinnamon hens

See also **fawn** and **recessive** and **sex-linked**.

clear   Canary devoid of any markings whatsoever. A clear can be a male or female, adult or unflighted, white, buff or yellow. It is possible to breed a cinnamon bird (cock or hen) which is completely devoid of all markings through melanin suppression. These birds are visually clears, but retain their genetic cinnamon characteristics. The same is true of a cinnamon carrier cock bird.

cock   Male canary (adult or unflighted).

colour feeding   Method of enhancing a bird's natural colour, displayed through its feather type. Colour feeding is only effective when the bird is moulting and the feathers are forming, enabling new growth to be coloured through the blood supply. This colouring will last until the bird next moults. Yorkshire canaries may be colour fed at the discretion of the fancier, with the exception of white ground colour birds, which should not be colour fed. Major exhibitions offer special classes for non colour-fed green birds, displaying their natural grass-green colour.

dark   Descriptive term applied to birds which display a large amount of variegation. Three parts dark describes a bird with 75 per cent dark plumage (with variegation, either green or cinnamon, blue or fawn) and only 25 per cent light-coloured plumage (buff, yellow or white).

evenly marked   Some exhibition canaries are classified by a system known as 'technical markings'. These markings touch a total of six 'technical points': both eyes, the flight feathers of both wings and both outer edges of the tail. Birds marked on opposite 'points' are termed 'evenly marked'. *See also* **technical mark/ point** and **uneven mark**.

factor   *See* **gene**.

fawn   Descriptive term applied to a white ground bird with inherent cinnamon characteristics. The bird can be a visual fawn or a non-visual fawn: that is, a clear bird which is either a full fawn (cinnamon) either cock or hen, or a cock bird which although not displaying the cinnamon (fawn) characteristic is capable of passing this factor to his offspring. *See also* **cinnamon**.

flighted   Term applied when a bird has completed its first adult moult, which includes the flight feathers in wings and tail. A flighted bird is a minimum of one year old, as the initial moult excludes these feathers. *See also* **adult** and **over-year** and **unflighted**.

foul   Canary which is displaying almost complete variegation throughout its plumage, resulting in an almost completely dark bird. This may be either a green, cinnamon, blue or fawn bird. Foul birds display light-coloured feathers (showing yellow or white ground colour) in the flight feathers of one wing only, or in the tail. Birds displaying more light feathers than this are classified as 'heavily variegated'. For exhibition purposes, special classes are usually provided at the larger specialist societies, for self (all dark) and foul green birds which have not been colour fed, and hence display their natural grass-green colour.

frosted/frosting Descriptive term applied to buff-feathered birds, deriving from the frosted appearance of the feather, which is caused because the colouring does not extend to the end of each feather tip, resulting in a frosted appearance when the feathers are laid together. *See also* **buff** and **mealy** and **silver**.

gamete *See* **germ cell**.

gene   In a germ cell, substance responsible for a given hereditary character.

germ cell   Sperm produced by the cock or ova produced by the hen.

gold   Victorian term to describe a bird displaying yellow feathering type. More commonly used in connection with Lizard canaries, but is also used in connection with white ground coloured Yorkshire canaries, particularly blues and fawns. *See also* **jonque** and **yellow**.

green   Canaries are capable of expressing two colour pigments or melanins, black and brown, which together combine to form 'green'

variegation when displayed on a yellow ground coloured bird. When both melanins are present in unmutated form, the bird is said to be a 'normal' and is capable of displaying only green variegation, and of passing this capability on to its offspring. The same pigments displayed on a white ground bird combine to form 'blue' variegation. Birds which are all dark are termed 'selfs', hence the expression 'self green' etc. *See also* **blue** and **normal**.

grizzle   Birds with fleck markings, usually on the head, forming a cap. For show purposes, a bird with a grizzled head (green marking), where the mark touches both eyes, is exhibited in the 'green marked' classes, as the mark is adjudged to touch two technical points. If the flecking touches only one eye, then the bird is exhibited in the class for 'clear or ticked' birds.

ground colour   Canaries commonly possess a yellow ground colour, on which the melanins of the plumage are overlaid, to produce a range of green and cinnamon ticks and markings. A mutation of yellow ground colour exists known as white ground colour, which removes yellow pigmentation from the feather. The same melanins which produce green and cinnamon markings on yellow ground birds, will produce blue and fawn coloration on white ground birds.

heavily variegated   A bird displaying more dark feathers (variegation) than light feathers (ground colour). For show purposes, different varieties of canary use different criteria concerning variegation, for example 'three parts dark' may apply to a Gloster canary, whilst in Yorkshire canaries the only marks (dark feathers) of concern are those touching any of the six technical points, and marks that do not touch these points are ignored. *See also* **lightly variegated**.

hen   Female canary, adult or unflighted.

in-breeding   Refers to the practice of pairing closely related birds together (father x daughter, mother x son, brother x sister) in order to try to 'fix' certain desirable characteristics. In-breeding is an extreme form of line breeding. *See also* **line breeding**.

jonque   Victorian term to describe a bird displaying yellow feathering type, now rarely used. *See also* **gold** and **yellow**.

juvenile   Bird which has not completed its initial moult, and hence still carries its juvenile or nest feathering.

lightly variegated   Bird displaying more light feathers (ground colour) than dark feathers (variegation). For exhibition purposes, remember that different rules will apply to different breeds of canary. *See also* **heavily variegated**.

line/line breeding   Method of pairing distantly related stock together, in order to establish a strong, true breeding family of birds. Typical pairings include grandfather x granddaughter, cousins, half brother x half sister etc. *See also* **in-breeding**.

marking   Loose term to describe an amount of variegation (either green, cinnamon, blue or fawn) on a bird.

mealy   Old-fashioned term dating back to Victorian times, describing a buff-feathered bird. *See also* **buff** and **frosted** and **silver.**

nest feather   Bird which has not completed its initial moult, and hence still carries its nest or juvenile feathering.

non-fed   Term which when applied to Yorkshire canaries, is used exclusively to describe self and foul green birds that have not been colour fed.

normal   Bird with both black and brown melanins present, in unmutated form. The melanins may be present in suppressed form, in which case the bird will not display any variegation, but nevertheless remains capable of passing on unmutated genes to its offspring. *See also* **blue** and **green**.

orange (Carophyll)   Carophyll orange is the most widely used colour food for type canaries. Orange blends together both carophyl red and carophyl yellow, giving a formulation for yellow ground coloured birds. It is easy to use during the annual moult, and does not burn the feathering as can be the case when using carophyl red. *See also* **Carophyll** and **red (Carophyll)**.

out-cross   The practice of pairing unrelated birds together.

over-year   Bird which has completed its first adult moult, and hence is over one year old. *See also* **adult** and **flighted**.

pedigree   The genetic background of the bird, which many breeders can trace for several generations.

pink-eyed   Term applied to a cinnamon or fawn bird (visual or non-visual), which cannot display black pigmentation, and hence has pink eyes in the nest, which darken to a deep burgundy colour as the bird matures.

point (technical)   Term referring to one of six points on the Yorkshire canary body that are classified as 'technical points', upon which the entire show classification is based. The technical points are both eyes, the flight feathers of both wings, and each outer side of the tail. Most other breeds use different (often much vaguer) criteria to describe markings, for example lightly variegated, heavily variegated, etc.

recessive   Genetic characteristic which is not necessarily displayed visually. Cinnamon is recessive to green, which is the natural plumage colour of the canary. When both green and cinnamon are present, then green takes precedence – it dominates the cinnamon factor, creating a recessive or hidden quality. *See also* **cinnamon** and **sex-linked**.

red (Carophyll)   A product specially formulated to enhance the colour of red canaries. Used by other colour-fed varieties such as Norwich and Yorkshire canaries, it can 'burn' the plumage (a term indicating an over-colouring of the feathering, turning what should be orange feathering into a purplish brown colour in extreme cases) if over-fed during the closing stages of the moult. It is therefore often overlooked in favour of carophyl orange, which is much easier to administer to yellow ground coloured birds. *See also* **Carophyll** and **orange (Carophyll)**.

red eyes   *See also* **cinnamon** and **pink-eyed**.

self   Bird which is totally dark, that is, the ground colour is not visible at all, because the bird displays 100 per cent variegation.

sex-linked   So named because the mode of inheritance follows that for sexual inheritance. Using cinnamon inheritance as an example, the cinnamon genes are carried on the X chromosome. The X and Y chromosomes are responsible for determining a canary's sex, and follow irrefutable laws of nature. Sex linking helps us understand exactly how the cinnamon gene will develop, and pre-determine the sex of any young birds in certain pairings.

silver   Victorian term to describe a bird displaying buff feathering type. It is more commonly used in connection with Lizard canaries, but is also used in connection with white ground coloured Yorkshire canaries, particularly blues and fawns.

soft moult   The term applied to an unseasonal, partial moult, which can quickly reduce the overall condition of the bird. A soft moult can be limited to a few body feathers, or can escalate to become almost an entire second moult, in severe cases.

strain   Loose term applied to a particular fancier's stud of birds, which have been line-bred for several generations.

technical mark/point   Marking system used primarily in Yorkshire canaries which are classified by a system known as 'technical markings'. These are markings which touch a total of six 'technical points', namely both eyes, the flight feathers of both wings and both outer edges of the tail. *See also* **buff** and **frosted** and **mealy**.

three-parts dark   Bird with 75 per cent of its plumage displaying variegation, and only 25 per cent displaying ground colour. *See also* **evenly marked** and **uneven mark**.

tick/ticked   A single marking, anywhere on the body, of any size. For show purposes, some canary breeds ignore ticks, whilst other apply sizes to the number of ticks displayed by the bird. In Yorkshires, unless the tick mark touches one of the six technical points, it is entirely ignored, and the bird will compete in the clear bird classes, unless the tick mark is cinnamon in colour, then it will compete in the cinnamon classes.

training   Exhibition canaries are schooled how to use the show cage from an early age, displaying to the best of their abilities when judged at exhibitions. This is known as 'show training' or 'training'.

uneven mark   Canary displaying irregular markings or markings touching one, three or five of the six technical points of its body. *See also* evenly marked and technical mark/ point.

unflighted   Term applied to a young bird, from leaving the nest to the completion of its first adult moult, which takes place approximately one year after it was born. The initial moult does not include the wing and tail flight feathers, hence the term 'unflighted'. *See also* **flighted**.

variegated   Visual pigmentation (melanins) of any colour, displayed anywhere on the bird.

X chromosome   The male sex chromosome, whilst the Y chromosome is the female sex chromosome. Hens carry one X and one Y chromosome, whilst cock birds carry two X chromosomes. Cock birds receive one X chromosome from their father and one from their mother, whilst hens receive the X chromosome from their father and the Y chromosome from their mother. In terms of sexual inheritance, hens determine the sex of all their offspring – the cock has no influence on this matter. *See also* **allele** and **chromosom**e.

Y chromosome   The female sex chromosome, whilst the X chromosome is the male sex chromosome. Hens carry one X and one Y chromosome, whilst cock birds carry two X chromosomes. Cock birds receive one X chromosome from their father and one from their mother, whilst hens receive the X chromosome from their father and the Y chromosome from their mother. In terms of sexual inheritance, hens determine the sex of all their offspring – the cock has no influence on this matter. *See also* **allele** and **chromosome**.

yellow   Describes a particular feather type. Yellow feathers are long and narrow, and the colouring extends to the feather tip, resulting in a dense, highly coloured appearance. Yellow birds are a bright lemon colour when not colour fed, deepening in shades up to a rich orange colour when colour fed. *See also* **gold** and **jonque**.

young   The progeny of adult canaries, a description often applied throughout the first year of the bird's life. A more proper term would be unflighted.

zygote   Single cell that forms the beginning of the new bird.

Further Information

POPULAR CANARY CLUBS

British Border Fancy Canary Club
R. S. Norman (Secretary)
3, Eskdale Close
Beechwood West
Runcorn
Cheshire WA7 2QX
www.bbfcc.co.uk
contact@bbfcc.co.uk

Fife Fancy Federation
C. Smith (Secretary)
61 Eastmead Avenue
Greenford
Middlesex UB6 9RF
www.igba.org.uk

International Gloster Breeders Association
Mr Malcolm Miles
33 Lambeth Drive
Stirchley
Telford
Shropshire TF3 1QW

Lizard Canary Association
J.D. Ross
30 Glenorrin Close
Lambton
Washington
Tyne & Wear NE38 0DZ
www.lizardcanary.co.uk

Norwich Canary Federation
K Ferry (Secretary)
31 Spencer Street
Ringstead
Northants NN14 4BX

Yorkshire Canary Club
J. Bannon (Secretary)
21 Orchard Grove
Bradford
West Yorkshire BD10 9BX
www.yccuk.com
jimbnnn@aol.com

OTHER USEFUL CONTACTS

The Canary Council UK
www.canarycouncil.co.uk

Cage & Aviary Birds
(weekly birdkeeping magazine)
www.cageandaviarybirds.com

For more information about the author and his work as a Yorkshire Canary champion breeder, visit www.yccuk.com/briankeenan or email briank857@gmail.com

Index